MW01515226

Alistair MacLean, the son of a Scots Minister, was brought up in the Scottish Highlands. In 1941 at the age of eighteen, he joined the Royal Navy; two-and-a-half years spent aboard a cruiser were later to give him the background for HMS *Ulysses*, his first novel, the outstanding documentary novel on the war at sea. After the war, he gained an English Honours degree at Glasgow University, and became a schoolmaster. In 1983, he was awarded a D.Litt. from the same university.

Alistair MacLean is now recognized to be the outstanding writer of our time in his own genre. He wrote twenty-nine world bestsellers. Many of his novels have been filmed – *The Guns of Navarone*, *Force 10 from Navarone*, *Where Eagles Dare* and *Bear Island* are among the most famous. He died in 1987.

BY THE SAME AUTHOR

ALISTAIR MACLEAN

Puppet on a Chain

HarperCollins *Publishers* India

a joint venture with

THE
INDIA
TODAY
GROUP

New Delhi

To Fred and Ina

HarperCollins *Publishers* India
a joint venture with
The India Today Group
by arrangement with
HarperCollins *Publishers* Limited

First published in William Collins Sons & Co. Ltd 1969

First published by HarperCollins *Publishers* India in 1997
Fourth impression 2004

Copyright © Alistair Maclean 1969

All rights reserved. No part of this publication may be reproduced,
stored in a retrieval system, or transmitted, in any form or by any
means, electronic, mechanical, photocopying, recording or otherwise,
without the prior permission of the publishers.

This book is sold subject to the condition that it shall not,
by way of trade or otherwise, be lent, resold, hired out or
otherwise circulated without the publisher's prior consent in
any form of binding or cover other than that in which it is
published and without a similar condition including this
condition being imposed on the subsequent purchaser.

HarperCollins *Publishers*
1A Hamilton House, Connaught Place, New Delhi 110 001, India
77-85 Fulham Palace Road, London W6 8JB, United Kingdom
Hazelton Lanes, 55 Avenue Road, Suite 2900, Toronto, Ontario M5R 3L2
and 1995 Markham Road, Scarborough, Ontario M1B 5M8, Canada
25 Ryde Road, Pymble, Sydney, NSW 2073, Australia
31 View Road, Glenfield, Auckland 10, New Zealand
10 East 53rd Street, New York NY 10022, USA

Printed and bound at
Thomson Press (India) Ltd.

CHAPTER ONE

'We shall be arriving in Schiphol Airport, Amsterdam, in just a few minutes.' Mellifluous, accentless, the Dutch stewardess's voice could have been precisely duplicated on any of a dozen European airlines. 'Please fasten your seat-belts and extinguish your cigarettes. We hope you have enjoyed your flight: we are sure you will enjoy your stay in Amsterdam.'

I'd spoken briefly to the stewardess on the way across. A charming girl, but given to a certain unwarranted optimism in her outlook on life in general and I had to take issue with her on two points: I hadn't enjoyed the flight and I didn't expect to enjoy my stay in Amsterdam. I hadn't enjoyed the flight because I hadn't enjoyed any flight since that day two years ago when the engines of a DC 8 had failed only seconds after take-off and led to the discovery of two things: that an unpowered jet has the gliding characteristics of a block of concrete and that plastic surgery can be very long, very painful, very expensive and occasionally not very successful. Nor did I expect to enjoy Amsterdam. even though it is probably the most beautiful city in the world with the friendliest inhabitants you'll find any-where: it's just that the nature of my business trips abroad automatically precludes the enjoyment of anything.

As the big KLM DC 8—I'm not superstitious, any plane can fall out of the sky—sank down, I glanced round its crowded interior. The bulk of the passengers, I observed, appeared to share my belief in the inherent madness of flying: those who weren't using their finger-nails to dig holes in KLM's upholstery were either leaning back with excessive nonchalance or chattering with the bright gay animation of those brave spirits who go to their impending doom with a quip on their smiling lips, the type who would have waved cheerfully to the admiring throngs as their tumbril drew up beside the guillotine. In short, a pretty

5

fair cross-section of humanity. Distinctly law-abiding. Definitely non-villainous. Ordinary: even nondescript.

Or perhaps that's unfair—the nondescript bit, I mean. To qualify for that rather denigrating description there must exist comparative terms of reference to justfy its use: unfortunately for the remainder of the passengers there were two others aboard that plane who would have made anyone look nondescript.

I looked at them three seats behind me on the other side of the aisle. This was hardly a move on my part to attract any attention as most of the men within eyeing distance of them had done little else but look at them since leaving Heathrow Airport: not to have looked at them at all would have been an almost guaranteed method of attracting attention.

Just a couple of girls sitting together. You can find a couple of girls sitting together almost anywhere but you'd have to give up the best years of your life to the search of finding a couple like those. One with hair as dark as a raven's wing, the other a shining platinum blonde, both clad, albeit marginally, in mini-dresses, the dark one in an all-white silk affair, the blonde all in black, and both of them possessed as far as one could see—and one could see a great deal—of figures that demonstrated clearly the immense strides forward made by a select few of womankind since the days of Venus di Milo. Above all, they were strikingly beautiful, but not with that vapid and empty brand of unformed good looks which wins the Miss World contest: curiously alike, they had the delicately formed bone structure, the cleanly cut .features, and the unmistakable quality of intelligence which would keep them still beautiful twenty years after the faded Miss Worlds of yesterday had long since given up the unequal competition.

The blonde girl smiled at me, a smile at once pert and provocative, but friendly. I gave her my impassive look, and as the trainee plastic surgeon who had worked his will on me hadn't quite succeeded in matching up the two sides of my face, my impassive expression is noticeably lacking in encouragement, but still she smiled at me. The dark girl

6

nudged her companion, who looked away from me, saw the reproving frown, made a face and stopped smiling. I looked away.

We were less than two hundred yards from the end of the runway now and to take my mind off the near-certainty of the undercarriage crumpling as soon as it touched the tarmac, I leaned back, closed my eyes and thought about the two girls. Whatever else I lacked, I reflected, no one could claim that I picked my assistants without regard to some of the more aesthetic aspects of life. Maggie, the dark girl, was twenty-seven and had been with me for over five years now: she was clever to just short of the point of being brilliant, she was methodical, painstaking, discreet, reliable and almost never made a mistake—in our business there is no such thing as a person who never makes mistakes. More important, Maggie and I were fond of each other and had been for years, an almost essential qualification where a momentary loss of mutual faith and interdependence could have consequences of an unpleasant and permanent nature: but we weren't, so far as I knew, too fond of each other, for that could have been equally disastrous.

Belinda, blonde, twenty-two, Parisian, half French, half English, on her first operational assignment, was an almost totally unknown quantity to me. Not an enigma, just unknown as a person: when the Sûreté lend you one of their agents, as they had lent Belinda to me, the accompanying dossier on that agent is so overwhelmingly comprehensive that no relevant fact in that person's background or past is left unmentioned. On a personal basis all I had been able to gather so far was that she was markedly lacking in that respect—if not unstinted admiration—that the young should accord to their elders and professional superiors, which in this case was myself. But she had about her that air of quietly resourceful competence which more than outweighed any reservations she might hold about her employer.

Neither girl had ever been to Holland before, which was one of the main reasons why they were accompanying me

7

there: apart from which, lovely young girls in our unlovely profession are rarer than fur coats in the Congo and hence all the more unlikely to attract the attention of the suspicious and the ungodly.

The DC 8 touched down, the undercarriage remained in one piece, so I opened my eyes and began to think of matters of more immediate urgency. Duclos. Jimmy Duclos was waiting to meet me at Schiphol Airport and Jimmy Duclos had something of importance and urgency to convey to me. Too important to send, even though coded, through normal channels of communication: too urgent to wait even for the services of a diplomatic courier from our embassy in The Hague. The probable content of the message I did not concern myself with: I'd know it in five minutes. And I knew it would be what I wanted. Duclos's sources of information were impeccable, the information itself always precise and one hundred per cent accurate. Jimmy Duclos never made mistakes—not, at least, of this nature.

The DC 8 was slowing down now and I could already see the crocodile disembarkation tube angling out from the side of the main building ready to line up with the plane's exit when it came to a halt. I unfastened my seatbelt, rose, glanced at Maggie and Belinda without expression or recognition and headed for the exit while the plane was still moving, a manoeuvre frowned upon by the airline authorities and certainly, in this case, by other passengers in the plane whose expressions clearly indicated that they were in the presence of a big-headed and churlish boor who couldn't wait to take his turn along with the rest of long-suffering and queueing mankind. I ignored them. I had long ago resigned myself to the realization that popularity was never to be my lot.

The stewardess smiled at me, though, but this was no tribute to either my appearance or personality. People smile at other people when they are impressed or apprehensive or both. Whenever I travel aboard a plane except when on holiday—which is about once every five years—I hand the stewardess a small sealed envelope for transmission to

8

the plane's captain and the captain, usually as anxious as the next man to impress a pretty girl, generally divulges the contents to her, which is a lot of fol-de-rol about complete priority under all circumstances and invariably wholly unnecessary except that it ensures one of impeccable and immediate lunch, dinner and bar service. Wholly necessary, though, was another privilege that several of my colleagues and I enjoyed—diplomatic-type immunity to Customs search, which was just as well as my luggage usually contained a couple of efficient pistols, a small but cunningly-designed kit of burglar's tools and some few other nefarious devices generally frowned upon by the immigration authorities of the more advanced countries. I never wore a gun aboard a plane, for apart from the fact that a sleeping man can inadvertently display a shoulder-holstered gun to a seat companion, thereby causing a whole lot of unnecessary consternation, only a madman would fire a gun within the pressurized cabin of a modern plane. Which accounts for the astonishing success of the sky-jackers: the results of implosion tend to be very permanent indeed.

The exit door opened and I stepped out into the corrugated disembarkation tube. Two or three airport employees politely stood to one side while I passed by and headed for the far end of the tube which debouched on to the terminal floor and the two contra-moving platforms which brought passengers to and from the immigration area.

There was a man standing at the end of the outward-bound moving platform with his back to it. He was of middle height, lean and a great deal less than prepossessing. He had dark hair, a deeply-trenched swarthy face, black cold eyes and a thin slit where his mouth should have been: not exactly the kind of character I would have encouraged to come calling on my daughter. But he was respectably enough dressed in a black suit and black overcoat and—although this was no criterion of respectability —was carrying a large and obviously brand-new airline bag.

But non-existent suitors for non-existent daughters were

no concern of mine. I'd moved far enough now to look up the outward-bound moving platform, the one that led to the terminal floor where I stood. There were four people on the platform and the first of them, a tall, thin, grey-suited man with a hairline moustache and all the outward indications of a successful accountant, I recognized at once. Jimmy Duclos. My first thought was that he must have considered his information to be of a vital and urgent nature indeed to come this length to meet me. My second thought was that he must have forged a police pass to get this far into the terminal and that made sense for he was a master forger. My third thought was that it would be courteous and friendly to give him a wave and a smile and so I did. He waved and smiled back.

The smile lasted for all of a second, then jelled almost instantly into an expression of pure shock. It was then I observed, almost sub-consciously, that the direction of his line of sight had shifted fractionally.

I turned round quickly. The swarthy man in the dark suit and coat no longer had his back to the travelator. He had come through 189° and was facing it now, his airline bag no longer dangling from his hand but held curiously high under his arm.

Still not knowing what was wrong, I reacted instinctively and jumped at the man in the black coat. At least, I started to jump. But it had taken me a whole long second to react and the man immediately—and I mean immediately— proceeded to demonstrate to both his and my total conviction that a second was what he regarded as being ample time to carry out any violent manoeuvre he wished. He'd been prepared, I hadn't, and he proved to be very violent indeed. I'd hardly started to move when he swung round in a viciously convulsive quarter-circle and struck me in the solar plexus with the edge of his airline bag.

Airline bags are usually soft and squashy. This one wasn't. I've never been struck by a pile-driver nor have any desire to be, but I can make a fair guess now as to what the feeling is likely to be. The physical effect was about the same. I collapsed to the floor as if some giant

10

hand had swept my feet from beneath me, and lay there motionless. I was quite conscious. I could see, I could hear, I could to some extent appreciate what was going on around me. But I couldn't even writhe, which was all I felt like doing at the moment. I'd heard of numbing mental shocks: this was the first time I'd ever experienced a totally numbing physical shock.

Everything appeared to happen in the most ridiculous slow motion. Duclos looked almost wildly around him but there was no way he could get off that travelator. To move backwards was impossible, for three men were crowded close behind him, three men who were apparently quite oblivious of what was going on—it wasn't until later, much later, that I realized that they must be accomplices of the man in the dark suit, put there to ensure that Duclos had no option other than to go forward with that moving platform and to his death. In retrospect, it was the most diabolically cold-blooded execution I'd heard of in a lifetime of listening to stories about people who had not met their end in the way their Maker had intended.

I could move my eyes, so I moved them. I looked at the airline bag and at one end, from under the flap, there protruded the colander-holed cylinder of a silencer. This was the pile-driver that had brought about my momentary paralysis—I hoped it was momentary—and from the force with which he had struck me I wondered he hadn't bent it into a U-shape. I looked up at the man who was holding the gun, his right hand concealed under the flap of the bag. There was neither pleasure nor anticipation in that swarthy face, just the calm certainty of a professional who knew how good he was at his job. Somewhere a disembodied voice announced the arrival of flight KL 132 from London—the plane we had arrived on. I thought vaguely and inconsequentially that I would never forget that flight number, but then it would have been the same no matter what flight I'd used for Duclos had been condemned to die before he could ever see me.

I looked at Jimmy Duclos and he had the face of a man condemned to die. His expression was desperate but it was

11

a calm and controlled desperation as he reached deep inside the hampering folds of his coat. The three men behind him dropped to the moving platform and again it was not until much later that the significance of this came upon me. Duclos's gun came clear of his coat and as it did there was a muted thudding noise and a hole appeared half-way down the left lapel of his coat. He jerked convulsively, then pitched forward and fell on his face: the travelator carried him on to the terminal area and his dead body rolled against mine.

I won't ever be certain whether my total inaction in the few seconds prior to Duclos's death was due to a genuine physical paralysis or whether I had been held in thrall by the inevitability of the way in which he died. It is not a thought that will haunt me for I had no gun and there was nothing I could have done. I'm just slightly curious, for there is no question that the touch of his dead body had an immediately revivifying effect upon me.

There was no miraculous recovery. Waves of nausea engulfed me and now that the initial shock of the blow was wearing off my stomach really started to hurt. My forehead ached, and far from dully, from where I must have struck my head on the floor as I had fallen. But a fair degree of muscular control had returned and I rose cautiously to my feet, cautiously because, due to the nausea and dizziness, I was quite prepared to make another involuntary return to the floor at any moment. The entire terminal area was swaying around in the most alarming fashion and I found that I couldn't see very well and concluded that the blow to my head must have damaged my eyesight, which was very odd as it had appeared to work quite effectively while I was lying on the floor. Then I realized that my eyelids were gumming together and an exploratory hand revealed the reason for this: blood, what briefly but wrongly appeared to me to be a lot of blood, was seeping down from a gash just on the hairline of the forehead. Welcome to Amsterdam, I thought, and pulled out a handkerchief: two dabs and my vision was twenty-twenty again.

From beginning to end the whole thing could have taken no more than ten seconds but already there was a crowd of anxious people milling around as always happens in cases like this: sudden death, violent death, is to man what the opened honey-pot is to bees—the immediate realization of the existence of either calls them forth in spectacular numbers from areas which, seconds previously, appeared to be devoid of all life.

I ignored them, as I ignored Duclos. There was nothing I could do for him now nor he for me, for a search of his clothes would have revealed nothing: like all good agents Duclos never committed anything of value to paper or tape but just filed it away in a highly-trained memory.

The dark and deadly man with the deadly gun would have made good his escape by this time: it was purely the routine and now ingrained instinct of checking even the uncheckable that made me glance towards the immigration area to confirm that he had indeed disappeared.

The dark man had not yet made good his escape. He was about two-thirds of the way along towards the immigration area, ambling unconcernedly along the in-bound moving platform, casually swinging his airline bag, and seemingly unaware of the commotion behind him. For a moment I stared at him, not comprehending, but only for a moment: this was the way the professional made good his escape. The professional pickpocket at Ascot who has just relieved the grey-top-hatted gentleman by his side of his wallet doesn't plunge away madly through the crowd to the accompaniment of cries of 'Stop thief' and the certainty of rapid apprehension: he is more likely to ask his victim his tip for the next race. A casual unconcern, a total normality, that was how the honours graduates in crime did it. And so it was with the dark man. As far as he was concerned I was the only witness to his action, for it was now that I belatedly realized for the first time the part the other three men had played in Duclos's death—they were still in the cluster of people round the dead man but there was nothing I or anybody else could ever prove against them. And, as far as the dark man knew, he'd left me in a state

13

in which I'd be unable to provide him with any trouble for some considerable time to come.

I went after him.

My pursuit didn't even begin to verge on the spectacular. I was weak, giddy and my midriff ached so wickedly that I found it impossible to straighten up properly, so that the combination of my weaving staggering run along that moving platform with my forward inclination of about thirty degrees must have made me look like nothing as much as a nonagenarian with lumbago in pursuit of God knows what.

I was half-way along the travelator, with the dark man almost at its end, when instinct or the sound of my running feet made him whirl round with the same catlike speed he'd shown in crippling me seconds before. It was immediately clear that he had no difficulty in distinguishing me from any nonagenarians he might have known, for his left hand immediately jerked up his airline bag while the right slid under the flap. I could see that what had happened to Duclos was going to happen to me—the travelator would discharge me or what was left of me to the floor at the end of its track: an ignominious way to die.

I briefly wondered what folly had prompted me, an unarmed man, to come in pursuit of a proven killer with a silenced pistol and was on the point of throwing myself flat on the platform when I saw the silencer waver and the dark man's unwinking gaze switch slightly to the left. Ignoring the probability of being shot in the back of the head, I swung round to follow his line of sight.

The group of people surrounding Duclos had temporarily abandoned their interest in him and transferred it to us: in view of what they must have regarded as my unhinged performance on the travelator it would have been odd if they hadn't. From the brief glance I had of their faces, their expressions ranged from astonishment to bafflement: there were no traces of understanding. Not in that particular knot of people. But there was understanding in plenty and a chilling purposefulness in the faces of the three men who had followed Duclos to his death: they

14

were now walking briskly up the in-bound travelator behind me, no doubt bent on following me to my death.

I heard a muffled exclamation behind me and turned again. The travelator had reached the end of its track, obviously catching the dark man off guard, for he was now staggering to retain his balance. As I would have expected of him by then he regained it very quickly, turned his back on me and began to run: killing a man in front of a dozen witnesses was a different matter entirely from killing a man in front of one unsupported witness, although I felt obscurely certain that he would have done so had he deemed it essential and the hell with the witnesses. I left the wondering why to later. I started to run again, this time with a deal more purpose, more like a lively septuagenarian.

The dark man, steadily outdistancing me, ran headlong through the immigration hall to the obvious confusion and consternation of the immigration officials, for people are not supposed to rush through immigration halls, they are supposed to stop, show their passports and give a brief account of themselves, which is what immigration halls are for. By the time it came to my turn to run the gamut, the dark man's hurried departure combined with my weaving staggering run and blood-streaked face had clearly alerted them to the fact that there was something amiss, for two of the immigration officials tried to detain me but I brushed by them—'brushed' was not the word they used in their later complaints—and passed through the exit door the dark man had just used.

At least, I tried to pass through it, but the damned door was blocked by a person trying to enter. A girl, that was all I'd the time or the inclination to register, just any girl. I dodged to the right and she dodged to the left, I dodged to my left, she dodged to her right. Check. You can see the same performance take place practically any minute on any city pavement when two over-polite people, each bent on giving the right of way to the other, side-step with such maladroit effectiveness that they succeed only in blocking each other's way: given the right circumstances where two really super-sensitive souls encounter each other the

15

whole embarrassing fandango can continue almost indefinitely.

I'm as quick an admirer of a well-executed *pas de deux* as the next man but I was in no mood to be detained indefinitely and after another bout of abortive side-stepping I shouted 'Get out of my damned way' and ensured that she did so by catching her by the shoulder and shoving her violently to one side. I thought I heard a bump and exclamation of pain, but I ignored it: I'd come back and apologize later.

I was back sooner than I expected. The girl had cost me not more than a few seconds, but those few seconds had been more than enough for the dark man. When I reached the concourse, the inevitably crowded concourse, there was no sign whatsoever of him, it would have been difficult to identify a Red Indian chief in full regalia among those hundreds of apparently aimlessly milling people. And it would be pointless to alert the airport security police, by the time I'd established my bona fides he'd be half-way to Amsterdam: even had I been able to get immediate action, their chances of apprehending the dark man would have been remote: highly skilled professionals were at work here, and such men always had the options on their escape routes wide open. I retraced my steps, this time at a leaden trudge, which was by now all I could muster. My head ached viciously but compared to the condition of my stomach I felt it would have been wrong to complain about my head. I felt awful and a glimpse of my pale and blood-smeared face in a mirror did nothing to make me feel any better.

I returned to the scene of my ballet performance where two large uniformed men, with holstered pistols, seized me purposefully by the arms.

'You've got the wrong man,' I said wearily, 'so kindly take your damned hands off me and give me room to breathe.' They hesitated, looked at each other, released me and moved away: they moved away nearly all of two inches. I looked at the girl who was being talked to gently by someone who must have been a very important

16

airport official for he wasn't wearing a uniform. I looked at the girl again because my eyes ached as well as my head and it was easier looking at her than at the man by her side.

She was dressed in a dark dress and dark coat with the white roll of a polo-necked jumper showing at the throat. She would have been about in her mid-twenties, and her dark hair, brown eyes, almost Grecian features and the olive blush to her complexion made it clear she was no native of those parts. Put her alongside Maggie and Belinda and you'd have to spend not only the best years of your life but also most of the declining ones to find a trio like them, although, admittedly, this girl was hardly looking at her best at that moment: her face was ashen and she was dabbing with a large white handkerchief, probably borrowed from the man at her side, at the blood oozing from an already swelling bruise on her left temple.

'Good God!' I said. I sounded contrite and I felt it for no more than the next man am I given to the wanton damaging of works of art. 'Did *I* do that?'

'Of course not.' Her voice was low and husky but maybe that was only since I'd knocked her down. 'I cut myself shaving this morning.'

'I'm terribly sorry. I was chasing a man who's just killed someone and you got in my way. I'm afraid he escaped.'

'My name is Schroeder. I work here.' The man by the girl's side, a tough and shrewd-looking character in perhaps his mid-fifties, apparently suffered from the odd self-depreciation which unaccountably afflicts so many men who have reached positions of considerable responsibility. 'We have been informed of the killing. Regrettable, most regrettable. That this should happen in Schiphol Airport!'

'Your fair reputation,' I agreed. 'I hope the dead man is feeling thoroughly ashamed of himself.'

'Such talk doesn't help,' Schroeder said sharply. 'Did you know the dead men?'

'How the hell should I? I've just stepped off the plane. Ask the stewardess, ask the captain, ask a dozen people

17

who were aboard the plane. KL 132 from London, arrival time 1555.' I looked at my watch. 'Good God! Only six minutes ago.'

'You haven't answered my question.' Schroeder not only looked shrewd, he was shrewd.

'I wouldn't know him even if I saw him now.'

'Mm. Has it ever occurred to you, Mr—ah—'

'Sherman.'

'Has it ever occurred to you, Mr Sherman, that normal members of the public don't set off in pursuit of an armed killer?'

'Maybe I'm sub-normal.'

'Or perhaps you carry a gun, too?'

I unbuttoned my jacket and held the sides wide.

'Did you—by any chance—recognize the killer?'

'No.' But I'd never forget him, though. I turned to the girl. 'May I ask you a question, Miss—'

'Miss Lemay,' Schroeder said shortly.

'Did you recognize the killer? You must have had a good look at him. Running men invariably attract attention.'

'Why should I know him?'

I didn't try to be shrewd as Schroeder had been. I said: 'Would you like to have a look at the dead man? Maybe might recognize *him*?'

She shuddered and shook her head.

Still not being clever, I said: 'Meeting someone?'

'I don't understand.'

'Your standing at the immigration exit.'

She shook her head again. If a beautiful girl can look ghastly, then she looked ghastly.

'Then why be here? To see the sights? I should have thought the immigration hall in Schiphol was the most unsightly place in Amsterdam.'

'That'll do.' Schroeder was brusque. 'Your questions are without point and the young lady is clearly distressed.' He gave me a hard look to remind me that I was responsible for her distress. 'Interrogation is for police officers.'

'I am a police officer.' I handed over my passport and warrant card and as I did Maggie and Belinda emerged from the exit. They glanced in my direction, broke step and stared at me with a mixture of concern and consternation as well they might considering the way I felt and undoubtedly looked, but I just scowled at them, as a self-conscious and injured man will scowl at anyone who stares at him, so they hurriedly put their faces straight again and moved on their way. I returned my attention to Schroeder, who was now regarding me with a quite different expression on his face.

'Major Paul Sherman, London Bureau of Interpol. This makes a considerable difference, I must say. It also explains why you behaved like a policeman and interrogate like a policeman. But I shall have to check your credentials, of course.'

'Check whatever you like with whoever you like,' I said, assuming that Mr Schroeder's English grammar wouldn't be up to picking faults in my syntax. 'I suggest you start with Colonel Van de Graaf at the Central HQ.'

'You know the Colonel?'

'It's just a name I picked out of my head. You'll find me in the bar.' I made to move off, then checked as the two big policemen made to follow me. I looked at Schroeder. 'I've no intention of buying drinks for them.'

'It's all right,' Schroeder said to the two men. 'Major Sherman will not run away.'

'Not as long as you have my passport and warrant card,' I agreed. I looked at the girl. 'I am sorry, Miss Lemay. This must have been a great shock to you and it's all my fault. Will *you* come and have a drink with me? You look as if you need one.'

She dabbed her cheek some more and looked at me in a manner that demolished all thoughts of instant friendship.

'I wouldn't even cross the road with you,' she said tonelessly. The way she said it indicated that she would willingly have gone half-way across a busy street with me and then abandoned me there. If I had been a blind man.

'Welcome to Amsterdam,' I said drearily and trudged off in the direction of the nearest bar.

CHAPTER TWO

I don't normally stay at five-star hotels for the excellent reason that I can't afford to, but when I'm abroad I have a practically unlimited expense account about which questions are seldom asked and never answered, and as those foreign trips tend to be exhausting affairs I see no reason to deny myself a few moments of peace and relaxation in the most comfortable and luxurious hotels possible.

The Hotel Rembrandt was undoubtedly one such. It was rather a magnificent if somewhat ornate edifice perched on a corner of one of the innermost ring canals of the old city: its splendidly carved balconies actually overhung the canal itself so that any careless sleepwalker could at least be reassured that he wouldn't break his neck if he toppled over the edge of his balcony—not, that is, unless he had the misfortune to land on top of one of the glass-sided canal touring boats which passed by at very frequent intervals: a superb eye-level view of those same boats could be had from the ground-floor restaurant which claimed, with some justification, to be the best in Holland.

My yellow Mercedes cab drew up at the front door and while I was waiting for the doorman to pay the cab and get my bag my attention was caught by the sound of 'The Skaters' Waltz' being played in the most excruciatingly off-key, tinny and toneless fashion I'd ever heard. The sound emanated from a very large, high, ornately painted and obviously very ancient mechanical barrel-organ parked across the road in a choice position to obstruct the maximum amount of traffic in that narrow street. Beneath the canopy of the barrel-organ, a canopy which appeared to have been assembled from the remnants of an unknown number of faded beach umbrellas, a row of puppets, beautifully made and, to my uncritical eye, exquisitely gowned in a variety of Dutch traditional costumes, jiggled up and down on the ends of rubber-covered springs: the motive power for the jiggling appeared to derive purely from the vibration inherent in the operation of this museum piece itself.

The owner, or operator, of this torture machine was a very old and very stooped man with a few straggling grey locks plastered to his head. He looked old enough to have built the organ himself when he was in his prime, but not, obviously, when he was in his prime as a musician. He held in his hand a long stick to which was attached a round tin can which he rattled continuously and was as continuously ignored by the passers-by he solicited, so I thought of my elastic expense account, crossed the street and dropped a couple of coins in his box. I can't very well say that he flashed me an acknowledging smile but he did give me a toothless grin and, as token of gratitude, changed into high gear and started in on the unfortunate Merry Widow. I retreated in haste, followed the porter and my bag up the vestibule steps, turned on the top step and saw that the ancient was giving me a very old-fashioned look indeed: not to be outdone in courtesy I gave him the same look right back and passed inside the hotel.

The assistant manager behind the reception desk was tall, dark, thin-moustached, impeccably tail-coated and his broad smile held all the warmth and geniality of that of a hungry crocodile, the kind of smile you knew would vanish instantly the moment your back was half-turned to him but which would be immediately in position, and more genuinely than ever, no matter how quickly you turned to face him again.

'Welcome to Amsterdam, Mr Sherman,' he said. 'We hope you will enjoy your stay.'

There didn't seem any ready reply to this piece of fatuous optimism so I just kept silent and concentrated on filling in the registration card. He took it from me as if I were handing him the Cullinan diamond and beckoned to a bell-boy, who came trotting up with my case, leaning over sideways at an angle of about twenty degrees.

'Boy! Room 616 for Mr Sherman.'

I reached across and took the case from the hand of the

far from reluctant 'boy'. He could have been—barely—the younger brother of the organ-grinder outside.

'Thank you.' I gave the bell-boy a coin. 'But I think I can manage.'

'But that case looks very heavy, Mr Sherman.' The assistant manager's protesting solicitude was even more sincere than his welcoming warmth. The case was, in fact, very heavy, all those guns and ammunition and metal tools for opening up a variety of things did tot up to a noticeable poundage, but I didn't want any clever character with clever ideas and even cleverer keys opening up and inspecting the contents of my bag when I wasn't around. Once inside an hotel suite there are quite a few places where small objects can be hidden with remote risk of discovery and the search is seldom assiduously pursued if the case is left securely locked in the first place. . . .

I thanked the assistant manager for his concern, entered the near-by lift and pressed the sixth-floor button. Just as the lift moved off I glanced through one of the small circular peephole windows inset in the door. The assistant manager, his smile now under wraps, was talking earnestly into a telephone.

I got out at the sixth floor. Inset in a small alcove directly opposite the lift gates was a small table with a telephone on it, and, behind the table, a chair with a young man with gold-embroidered livery in it. He was an unprepossessing young man, with about him that vague air of indolence and insolence which is impossible to pin down and about which complaint only makes one feel slightly ridiculous: such youths are usually highly-specialized practitioners in the art of injured innocence.

'Six-one-six?' I asked.

He crooked a predictably languid thumb. 'Second door along.' No 'sir', no attempt to get to his feet. I passed up the temptation to clobber him with his own table and instead promised myself the tiny, if exquisite, pleasure of dealing with him before I left the hotel.

I asked: 'You the floor-waiter?'

He said, 'Yes, sir,' and got to his feet. I felt a twinge of disappointment.

'Get me some coffee.'

I'd no complaints with 616. It wasn't a room, but a rather sumptuous suite. It consisted of a hall, a tiny but serviceable kitchen, a sitting-room, bedroom and bathroom. Both sitting-room and bedroom had doors leading on to the same balcony. I made my way out there.

With the exception of an excruciating, enormous and neon-lit monstrosity of a sky-high advertisement for an otherwise perfectly innocuous cigarette, the blaze of coloured lights coming up over the darkening streets and skline of Amsterdam belonged to something out of a fairy tale, but my employers did not pay me—and give me that splendid expense allowance—just for the privilege of mooning over any city skyline, no matter how beautiful. The world I lived in was as remote from the world of fairy tales as the most far-flung galaxy on the observable rim of the universe. I turned my attention to more immediate matters.

I looked down towards the source of the far from muted traffic roar that filled all the air around. The broad highway directly beneath me—and about seventy feet beneath me—appeared to be inextricably jammed with clanging tram-cars, hooting vehicles and hundreds upon hundreds of motor-scooters and bicycles, all of whose drivers appeared to be bent on instant suicide. It appeared inconceivable that any of those two-wheeled gladiators could reasonably expect any insurance policy covering a life expectancy of more than five minutes, but they appeared to regard their imminent demise with an insouciant bravado which never fails to astonish the newcomer to Amsterdam. As an afterthought, I hoped that if anyone was going to fall or be pushed from the balcony it wasn't going to be me.

I looked up. Mine was obviously—as I had specified—the top storey of the hotel. Above the brick wall separating my balcony from that of the suite next door, there was some sort of stone-carved baroque griffin supported on a

23

stone pier. Above that again—perhaps thirty inches above—ran the concrete coaming of the roof. I went inside.

I took from the inside of the case all the things I'd have found acutely embarrassing to be discovered by other hands. I fitted on a felt-upholstered underarm pistol which hardly shows at all if you patronize the right tailor, which I did, and tucked a spare magazine in a back trouser pocket. I'd never had to fire more than one shot from that gun, far less have to fall back on the spare magazine, but you never know, things were getting worse all the time. I then unrolled the canvas-wrapped array of burglarious instruments—this belt again, and with the help of an understanding tailor again, is invisible when worn round the waist—and from this sophisticated plethora extracted a humble but essential screwdriver. With this I removed the back of the small portable fridge in the kitchen—it's surprising how much empty space there is behind even a small fridge—and there cached all I thought it advisable to cache. Then I opened the door to the corridor. The floor-waiter was still at his post.

'Where's my coffee?' I asked. It wasn't exactly an angry shout but it came pretty close to it.

This time I had him on his feet first time out.

'It come by dumb-waiter. Then I bring.'

'You better bring fast.' I shut the door. Some people never learn the virtues of simplicity, the dangers of over-elaboration. His phoney attempts at laboured English were as unimpressive as they were pointless.

I took a bunch of rather oddly shaped keys from my pocket and tried them, in succession, on the other door. The third fitted—I'd have been astonished if none had. I pocketed the keys, went to the bathroom and had just turned the shower up to maximum when the outer door-bell rang, followed by the sound of the door opening. I turned off the shower, called to the floor-waiter to put the coffee on the table and turned the shower on again. I hoped that the combination of the coffee and the shower might persuade whoever required to be persuaded that here was

24

a respectable guest unhurriedly preparing for the leisurely evening that lay ahead but I wouldn't have bet pennies on it. Still, one can but try.

I heard the outer door close but left the shower running in case the waiter was leaning his ear against the door—he had the look about him of a man who would spend much of his time leaning against doors or peering through keyholes. I went to the front door and stooped. He wasn't peering through this particular keyhole. I opened the door fractionally, taking my hand away, but no one fell into the hallway, which meant that either no one had any reservations about me or that someone had so many that he wasn't going to run any risks of being found out: a great help either way. I closed and locked the door, pocketed the bulky hotel key, poured the coffee down the kitchen sink, turned off the shower and left via the balcony door: I had to leave it wide open, held back in position by a heavy chair: for obvious reasons, few hotel balcony doors have a handle on the outside.

I glanced briefly down to the street, across at the windows of the building opposite, then leaned over the concrete balustrade and peered to left and right to check if the occupants of the adjoining suites were peering in my direction. They weren't. I climbed on to the balustrade, reached for the ornamental griffin so grotesquely carved that it presented a number of excellent handholds, then reached for the concrete coaming of the roof and hauled myself up top. I don't say I liked doing it but I didn't see what else I could do.

The flat grass-grown roof was, as far as could be seen, deserted. I rose and crossed to the other side, skirting TV aerials, ventilation outlets and those curious miniature green-houses which in Amsterdam serve as skylights, reached the other side and peered cautiously down. Below was a very narrow and very dark alley, for the moment, at least, devoid of life. A few yards to my left I located the fire-escape and descended to the second floor. The escape door was locked, as nearly all such doors are from the inside, and the lock itself was of the double-action type, but

25

no match for the sophisticated load of ironmongery I carried about with me.

The corridor was deserted. I descended to the ground floor by the main stairs because it is difficult to make a cautious exit from a lift which opens on to the middle of the reception area. I needn't have bothered. There was no sign of the assistant manager, the bell-boy or the doorman and, moreover, the hall was crowded with a new batch of plane arrivals besieging the reception desk. I joined the crowd at the desk, politely tapped a couple of shoulders, reached an arm through, deposited my room key on the desk, walked unhurriedly to the bar, passed as unhurriedly through it and went out by the side entrance.

Heavy rain had fallen during the afternoon and the streets were still wet, but there was no need to wear the coat I had with me so I carried it slung over my arm and strolled along hatless, looking this way and that, stopping and starting again as the mood took me, letting the wind blow me where it listeth, every inch, I hoped, the tourist sallying forth for the first time to savour the sights and sounds of night-time Amsterdam.

It was while I was ambling along the Herengracht, dutifully admiring the façades of the houses of the merchant princes of the seventeenth century, that I first became sure of this odd tingling feeling in the back of the neck. No amount of training or experience will ever develop this feeling. Maybe it has something to do with ESP. Maybe not. Either you're born with it or you aren't. I'd been born with it.

I was being followed.

The Amsterdamers, so remarkably hospitable in every other way, are strangely neglectful when it comes to providing benches for their weary visitors—or their weary citizens, if it comes to that—along the banks of their canals. If you want to peer out soulfully and restfully over the darkly gleaming waters of their night-time canals the best thing to do is to lean against a tree, so I leaned against a convenient tree and lit a cigarette.

I stood there for several minutes, communing, so I hoped it would seem, with myself, lifting the cigarette occasionally, but otherwise immobile. Nobody fired silenced pistols at me, nobody approached me with a sandbag preparatory to lowering me reverently into the canal. I'd given him every chance but he'd taken no advantage of it. And the dark man in Schiphol had had me in his sights but hadn't pulled the trigger. Nobody wanted to do away with me. Correction. Nobody wanted to do away with me yet. It was a crumb of comfort, at least.

I straightened, stretched and yawned, glancing idly about me, a man awakening from a romantic reverie. He was there all right, not leaning as I was with my back to the tree but with his shoulder to it so that the tree stood between him and myself, but it was a very thin tree and I could clearly distinguish his front and rear elevations.

I moved on and turned right into the Leidestraat and dawdled along this doing some inconsequential window-shopping as I went. At one point I stepped into a shop doorway and gazed at some pictorial exhibits of so highly intrinsic an artistic nature that, back in England, they'd have had the shop-owner behind bars in nothing flat. Even more interestingly, the window formed a near-perfect mirror. He was about twenty yards away now, peering earnestly into the shuttered window of what might have been a fruit shop. He wore a grey suit and a grey sweater and that was all that could be said about him: a grey nondescript anonymity of a man.

At the next corner I turned right again, past the flower market on the banks of the Singel canal. Half-way along I stopped at a stall, inspected the contents, and bought a carnation: thirty yards away the grey man was similarly inspecting a stall but either he was mean-souled or hadn't an expense account like mine, for he bought nothing, just stood and looked.

I had thirty yards on him and when I turned right again into the Vijzelstraat I strode along very briskly indeed until I came to the entrance of an Indonesian restaurant. I turned in, closing the door behind me. The doorman, obviously a pensioner, greeted me civilly enough but made no attempt to rise from his stool.

I looked through the door and within just a few seconds the grey man came by. I could see now that he was more elderly than I had thought, easily in his sixties, and I must admit that for a man of his years he was putting up a remarkable turn of speed. He looked unhappy.

I put on my coat and mumbled an apology to the doorman. He smiled and said 'Good night' as civilly as he had said 'Good evening'. They were probably full up anyway. I went outside, stood in the doorway, took a folded trilby from one pocket and a pair of wire spectacles from the other and put them both on. Sherman, I hoped, transformed.

He was about thirty yards distant now, proceeding with a curious scuttling action, stopping every now and again to peer into a doorway. I took life and limb in hand, launched myself across the street and arrived at the other side intact but unpopular. Keeping a little way behind, I paralleled the grey man for about another hundred yards when he stopped. He hesitated, then abruptly began to retrace his steps, almost running now, but this time stopping to go inside every place that was open to him. He went into the restaurant I'd so briefly visited and came out in ten seconds. He went in the side entrance of the Hotel Carlton and emerged from the front entrance, a detour that could not have made him very popular as the Hotel Carlton does not care overmuch for shabby old men with roll-neck sweaters using their foyer as a short cut. He went into another Indonesian restaurant at the end of the block and reappeared wearing the chastened expression of a man who has been thrown out. He dived into a telephone-box and when he emerged he looked more chastened than ever. From there he took up his stance on the central reservation tram stop on the Muntplein .I joined the queue.

The first tram along, a three-coach affair, bore the number '16' and the destination board 'Central Station'. The grey man boarded the first coach. I entered the
28

second and moved to the front seat where I could keep a watchful eye on him, at the same time positioning myself so as to present as little as possible of myself to his view should he begin to interest himself in his fellow passengers. But I needn't have worried; his lack of interest in his fellow passengers was absolute. From the continual shift and play of expression, all unhappy, on his face, and the clasping and unclasping of his hinds,˙ here clearly was a man with other and more important things on his mind, not least of which was the degree of sympathetic under-standing he could expect from his employers.

The man in grey got off at the Dam. The Dam, the main square in Amsterdam, is full of historical landmarks such as the Royal Palace and the New Church which is so old that they have to keep shoring it up to prevent it from collapsing entirely, but neither received as much as a glance from the grey man that night. He scuttled down a side-street by the Hotel Krasnapolsky, turned left, in the direction of the docks, along the Oudezijds Voorburgwal canal, then turned right again and dipped into a maze of side-streets that obviously penetrated more and more deeply into the warehouse area of the town, one of the few areas not listed among the tourist attractions of Amsterdam. He was the easiest man to follow I'd ever come across. He looked neither to left nor right, far less behind him. I could have been riding an elephant ten paces behind him and he'd never have noticed.

I stopped at a corner and watched him make his way along a narrow, ill-lit and singularly unlovely street, lined exclusively by warehouses on both sides, tall five-storey buildings whose gabled roofs leaned out towards those on the other side of the street, lending an air of claustrophobic menace, of dark foreboding and brooding watchfulness which I didn't much care for at all.

From the fact that the grey man had now broken into a shambling run I concluded that this excessive demonstration of zeal could only mean that he was near journey's end, and I was right. Half-way along the street he ran up a set of handrailed steps, produced a key, opened a door and disappeared inside a warehouse. I followed at my leisure, but not too slowly, and glanced incuriously at the nameplate above the door of the warehouse: 'Morgenstern and Muggenthaler', the legend read. I'd never heard of the firm, but it was a name I'd be unlikely to forget. I passed on without breaking step.

It wasn't much of an hotel room, I had to admit, but then it wasn't much of an hotel to begin with. Just as the outside of the hotel was small and drab and paint-peeling and unprepossessing, so was the interior of the room. The few articles of furniture the room contained, which included a single bed and a sofa which obviously converted into a bed, had been sadly overtaken by the years since the long-dead days of their prime, if they'd ever had a prime. The carpet was threadbare, but nowhere near as threadbare as the curtains and bed coverlet: the tiny bathroom leading off the room had the floor space of a telephone-box. But the room was saved from complete disaster by a pair of redeeming features that would have lent a certain aura of desirability to even the bleakest of prison cells. Maggie and Belinda, perched side by side on the edge of the bed, looked at me without enthusiasm as I lowered myself wearily on to the couch.

'Tweedledum and Tweedledee.' I said. 'All alone in wicked Amsterdam. Everything all right?'

'No.' There was a positive note in Belinda's voice.

'No?' I let my surprise show.

She gestured to indicate room. 'Well, I mean, look at it.'

I looked at it. 'So?'

'Would *you* live here?'

'Well, frankly, no. But then five-star hotels are for managerial types like myself. For a couple of struggling typists these quarters are perfectly adequate. For a couple of young girls who are not the struggling typists they appear to be this provides about as complete a degree of anonymity of background as you can hope to achieve.' I paused. 'At least, I hope. I *assume* you're both in the clear. Anyone on the plane you recognized?'

'No.' They spoke in unison with an identical shake of the head.

'Anyone in Schiphol you recognized?'

'No.'

'Anyone take any particular interest in you at Schiphol?'

'No.'

'This room bugged?'

'No.'

'Been out?'

'Yes.'

'Been followed?'

'No.'

'Room searched in your absence?'

'No.'

'You look amused, Belinda, ' I said. She wasn't exactly giggling but she was having a little difficulty with her facial muscles. 'Do tell. I need cheering up.'

'Well.' She was suddenly thoughtful, perhaps recalling that she hardly knew me at all. 'Nothing. I'm sorry.'

'Sorry about what, Belinda?' An avuncular and encouraging tone which had the odd effect of making her wriggle uncomfortably.

'Well, all those cloak-and-dagger precautions for a couple of girls like us. I don't see the need—'

'Do be quiet, Belinda!' That was Maggie, quicksilver as ever in the old man's defence though God knew why. I'd had my professional successes that, considered by themselves, totted up to a pretty impressive list but a list that, compared to the quota of failures, paled into a best-forgotten insignificance. 'Major Sherman,' Maggie went on severely, 'always knows what he is doing.'

'Major Sherman,' I said frankly, 'would give his back teeth to believe in that.' I looked at them speculatively. 'I'm not changing the subject, but how about some of the old commiseration for the wounded master?'

'We know our place,' Maggie said primly. She rose, peered at my forehead and sat down again. 'Mind you, it does seem a very small piece of sticking plaster for what seemed such a lot of blood.'

'The managerial classes bleed easily, something to do with sensitive skins, I understand. You heard what happened?'

Maggie nodded. 'This dreadful shooting, we heard you tried—'

'To intervene. Tried, as you so rightly said.' I looked at Belinda. 'You must have found it terribly impressive, first time out with your new boss and he gets clobbered the moment he sets foot in a foreign country.'

She glanced involuntarily at Maggie, blushed—platinum blondes of the right sort blush very easily—and said defensively: 'Well, he was too quick for you.'

'He was all of that,' I agreed. 'He was also too quick for Jimmy Duclos.'

'Jimmy Duclos?' They had a gift for speaking in unison.

'The dead man. One of our very best agents and a friend of mine for many years. He had urgent and, I assume, vital information that he wished to deliver to me in person in Schiphol. I was the only person in England who knew he would be there. But someone in this city knew. My rendezvous with Duclos was arranged through two completely unconnected channels, but someone not only knew I was coming but also knew the precise flight and time and so was conveniently on hand to get to Duclos before he could get to me. You will agree, Belinda, that I wasn't changing the subject? You will agree that if they knew that much about me and one of my associates, they may be equally well informed about some other of my associates.'

They looked at each other for a few moments, then Belinda said in a low voice: 'Duclos was one of us?'

'Are you deaf?' I said irritably.

'And that we—Maggie and myself, that is—'

'Precisely.'

They seemed to take the implied threats to their lives fairly calmly, but then they'd been trained to do a job and were here to do a job and not fall about in maidenly swoons. Maggie said: 'I'm sorry about your friend.'

I nodded.

'And I'm sorry if I was silly,' Belinda said. She meant it

too, all contrition, but it wouldn't last. She wasn't the type. She looked at me, extraordinary green eyes under dark eyebrows and said slowly: 'They're on to you, aren't they?'

'That's my girl,' I said approvingly. 'Worrying about her boss. On to me? Well, if they're not they have half the staff at the Hotel Rembrandt keeping tabs on the wrong man. Even the side entrances are watched: I was tailed when I left tonight.'

'He didn't follow you far.' Maggie's loyalty could be positively embarrassing.

'He was incompetent and obvious. So are the others there. People operating on the fringes of junky-land frequently are. On the other hand they may be deliberately trying to provoke a reaction. If that's their intention, they're going to be wildly successful.'

'Provocation?,' Maggie sounded sad and resigned. Maggie knew me.

'Endless. Walk, run, or stumble into everything. With both eyes tightly shut.'

'This doesn't seem a very clever or scientific way of investigation to me,' Belinda said doubtfully. Her contrition was waning fast.

'Jimmy Duclos was clever. The cleverest we had. And scientific. He's in the city mortuary.'

Belinda looked at me oddly. 'You will put your neck under the block?'

'On the block, dear,' Maggie said absently. 'And don't go on telling your new boss what he can and can't do.' But her heart wasn't in her words for the worry was in her eyes.

'It's suicide,' Belinda persisted.

'So? Crossing the streets in Amsterdam is suicide—or looks like it. Tens of thousands of people do it every day.' I didn't tell them that I had reason to believe that my early demise did not head the list of the ungodly priorities, not because I wished to improve my heroic image, but because it would only lead to the making of more explanations which I did not at the moment wish to make.

'You didn't bring us here for nothing,' Maggie said.

'That's so. But any toe-tramping is my job. You keep

33

out of sight. Tonight, you're free. Also tomorrow, except that I want Belinda to take a walk with me tomorrow evening. After that, if you're both good girls, I'll take you to a naughty night-club.'

'I come all the way from Paris to go to a naughty night-club?' Belinda was back at being amused again. 'Why?'

'I'll tell you why. I'll tell you some things about night-clubs you don't know. I'll tell you why we're here. In fact,' I said expansively, 'I'll tell you everything.' By 'everything' I meant everything I thought they needed to know, not everything there was to tell: the differences were considerable. Belinda looked at me with anticipation. Maggie with a wearily affectionate scepticism, but then Maggie knew me. 'But first, some Scotch.'

'We have no Scotch, Major.' Maggie had a very puritanical side to her at times.

'Not even au fait with the basic principles of intelligence. You must learn to read the right books.' I nodded to Belinda. 'The phone. Get some. Even the managerial classes must relax occasionally.'

Belinda stood up, smoothing down her dark dress and looking at me with a sort of puzzled disfavour. She said slowly: 'When you spoke about your friend in the mortuary I watched and you showed nothing. He's still there and now you are—what is the word—flippant. Relaxing, you say. How can you do this?'

'Practice. And a siphon of soda.'

CHAPTER THREE

It was classical night that night at the Hotel Rembrandt
with the barrel-organ giving forth a rendition of an
excerpt from Beethoven's Fifth that would have had the
old composer down on his knees giving eternal thanks for
his almost total deafness. Even at fifty yards, the distance
from which I was prudently observing through the now
gently drizzling rain, the effect was appalling: it was an
extraordinary tribute to the tolerance of the people of
Amsterdam, city of music-lovers and home of the world-
famous Concertgebouw, that they didn't lure the elderly
operator into a convenient tavern and, in his absence,
trundle his organ into the nearest canal. The ancient was
still rattling his can at the end of his stick, a purely reflex
action for there was no one about that night, not even
the doorman, who had either been driven inside by the
rain or was a music-lover.

I turned down the side-street by the bar entrance. There
was no figure lurking about adjacent doorways or in the
entrance to the bar itself, nor had I expected to find any. I
made my way round to the alley and the fire-escape, climbed
up to the roof, crossed it and located the stretch of
coaming that directly overhung my own balcony.

I peered over the edge. I could see nothing, but I could
smell something. Cigarette smoke, but not emanating from
a cigarette made by one of the more reputable tobacco
companies, who don't include reefers among their market-
able products. I leaned further out to almost the point of
imbalance and then I could see things, not much, but
enough: two pointed toe-caps and, for a moment, the
arcing, glowing tip of a cigarette, obviously on the down-
swing of an arm.

I withdrew in caution and with silence, rose, re-crossed
to the fire-escape, descended to the sixth-floor, let myself
through the fire-escape door, locked it again, walked quietly

35

along to the door of Room 616 and listened. Nothing. I opened the door quietly with the skeleton I'd tried earlier and went inside, closing the door as quickly as I could: otherwise indetectable draughts can eddy cigarette smoke in a way to attract the attention of the alert smoker. Not that junkies are renowned for their alertness.

This one was no exception. Predictably enough, it was the floor-waiter. He was sitting comfortably in an armchair, feet propped up on the balcony sill, smoking a cigarette in his left hand: his right lay loosely on his knee and cradled a gun.

Normally, it is very difficult to approach anyone, no matter how soundlessly, from behind without some form of sixth sense giving them warning of your approach: but many drugs have a depressive influence on this instinct and what the floor-waiter was smoking was one of them.

I was behind him with my gun at his right ear and he still didn't know I was there. I touched him on the right shoulder. He swung round with a convulsive jerk of his body and cried out in pain as his movement gouged the barrel of my gun into his right eye. He lifted both hands to his momentarily injured eye and I took the gun from him without resistance, pocketed it, reached for his shoulder and jerked hard. The waiter catapulted over backwards, completing a somersault, and landing very heavily on his back and the back of his head. For maybe ten seconds he lay there, quite dazed, then propped himself up on one arm. He was making a curious hissing sound, his bloodless lips had vanished to reveal tobacco-stained teeth set in a vulpine snarl and his eyes were dark with hate. I didn't see much chance of our having a friendly get-together.

'We do play rough, don't we?' he whispered. Junkies are great patronizers of the violent cinema and their dialogue is faultless.

'Rough?' I was surprised. 'Oh, dear me, no. Later we play rough. If you don't talk.' Maybe I went to the same cinema as he did. I picked up the cigarette that lay smouldering on the carpet, sniffed at it in disgust and squashed it out in an ashtray. The waiter rose unsteadily, still shaken and unsteady on his feet, and I didn't believe any of it. When he spoke again, the snarl had gone from his face and voice. He had decided to play it cool, the calm before the storm, an old and worn-out script, maybe we should both start attending the opera instead.

'What would you like to talk about?' he asked.

'About what you're doing in my room for a start. And who sent you here.'

He smiled wearily. 'The law has already tried to make me tell things. I know the law. You can't make me talk. I've got my rights. The law says so.'

'The law stops right outside my front door here. This side of that door we're both beyond the law. You know that. In one of the great civilized cities of the world you and I are living in our own little jungle. But there's a law there too. Kill or be killed.'

Maybe it was my own fault for putting ideas in his head. He dived hard and low to get under my gun but not low enough for his chin to get under my knee. It hurt my knee quite badly and by that token should have laid him out, but he was tough, grabbed at the only leg I had left in contact with the ground and brought us both down. My gun went spinning and we rolled about on the floor for a bit, belabouring each other enthusiastically. He was a strong boy, too, as strong as he was tough, but he laboured under two disadvantages: a strict training on marijuana had blunted the honed edge of his physical fitness, and though he had a highly developed instinct for dirty fighting he'd never really been trained to it. By and by we were on our feet again with my left hand pushing his right wrist somewhere up between his shoulder-blades.

I pushed his wrist higher and he screamed as if in agony, which he might well have been as his shoulder was making a peculiar cracking noise, but I couldn't be sure so I pushed a bit higher and removed all doubt, then thrust him out on to the balcony in front of me and forced him over the balustrade until his feet were clear of the ground and he was hanging on to the balustrade with his free left hand as if his life depended on it, which indeed it did.

'You an addict or a pusher?' I enquired.

He mouthed an obscenity in Dutch, but I know Dutch, including all the words I shouldn't. I put my right hand over his mouth for the sort of sound he was about to make could be heard even above the roar of the traffic, and I didn't want to alarm the citizens of Amsterdam un- necessarily. I eased the pressure and removed my hand.

'Well?'

'A pusher.' His voice was a sobbing croak. 'I sell them.'

'Who sent you?'

'No! No! No!'

'Your decision. When they pick what's left of you from the pavement there they'll think you're just another cannabis smoker who got too high and took a trip into the wild blue yonder.'

'That's murder!' He was still sobbing, but his voice was only a husky whisper now, maybe the view was making him dizzy. 'You wouldn't—'

'Wouldn't I? Your people killed a friend of mine this afternoon. Exterminating vermin can be a pleasure. Seventy feet's a long drop—and not a mark of violence. Except that every bone in your body will be broken. Seventy feet. Look!'

I heaved him a bit further over the balustrade so that he could have a better look and had to use both hands to haul him back again.

'Talk?'

He made a hoarse sound in his throat, so I hauled him off the balustrade and pushed him inside to the centre of the room. I said, 'Who sent you?'

I've said he was tough, but he was a great deal tougher than I had ever imagined. He should have been fear- stricken and in agony, and I have no doubt that he was both, but that didn't stop him from whirling round convulsively to his right in a full circle and breaking free from my grip. The sheer unexpectedness of it had caught me off guard. He came at me again, a knife that had suddenly appeared in his left hand curving upwards in a wicked arc and aimed for a point just below the breast-bone. Normally, he would probably have done a nice job of carving but the circumstances were abnormal: his timing and reactions were gone. I caught and clamped his knife wrist in both my hands, threw myself backwards, straightened a leg under him as I jerked his arm down and sent him catapulting over me. The thud of his landing shook the room and probably quite a few adjacent rooms at that.

I twisted and got to my feet in one motion but the need for haste was gone. He was on the floor on the far side of the room, his head resting on the balcony sill. I lifted him by his lapels and his head lolled back till it almost touched his shoulder-blades. I lowered him to the floor again. I was sorry he was dead, because he'd probably had information that could have been invaluable to me, but that was the only reason I was sorry.

I went through his pockets, which held a good number of interesting articles but only two that were of interest to me: a case half full of handmade reefers and a couple of scraps of paper. One paper bore the typed letters and figures MOO 144, the other two numbers—910020 and 2789. Neither meant a thing to me but on the reasonable assumption that the floor-waiter wouldn't have been carrying them on his person unless they had some significance for him I put them away in a safe place that had been provided for me by my accommodating tailor, a small pocket that had been let into the inside of the right trouser-leg about six inches above the ankle.

I tidied up what few signs of struggle there had been, took the dead man's gun, went out on the balcony, leaned out over the balustrade and spun the gun upwards and to the left. It cleared the coaming and landed soundlessly on the roof about twenty feet away. I went back inside, flushed the reefer end down the toilet, washed the ashtray and opened every door and window to let the sickly smell evaporate as soon as possible. Then I dragged the waiter

39

across to the tiny hall and opened the door on to the passage.

The hallway was deserted. I listened intently, but could hear nothing, no sound of approaching footfalls. I crossed to the lift, pressed the button, waited for the lift to appear, opened the door a crack, inserted a matchbox between jamb and door so that the latter couldn't close and complete the electrical circuit then hurried back to my suite. I dragged the waiter across to the lift, opened the door, dumped him without ceremony on the lift floor, withdrew the matchbox and let the door swing to. The lift remained where it was: obviously, no one was pressing the button of that particular lift at that particular moment.

I locked the outside door to my suite with the skeleton and made my way back to the fire-escape, by now an old and trusted friend. I reached street level unobserved and made my way round to the main entrance. The ancient at the barrel-organ was playing Verdi now and Verdi was losing by a mile. The operator had his back to me as I dropped a guilder into his tin can. He turned to thank me, his lips parted in a toothless smile, then he saw who it was and his jaw momentarily dropped open. He was at the very bottom of the heap and no one had bothered to inform him that Sherman was abroad. I gave him a kindly smile and passed into the foyer.

There were a couple of uniformed staff behind the desk, together with the manager, whose back was at the moment towards me. I said loudly: 'Six-one-six, please.'

The manager turned round sharply, his eyebrows raised high but not high enough. Then he gave me his warm-hearted crocodile smile.

'Mr Sherman. I didn't know you were out.'

'Oh yes, indeed. Pre-dinner constitutional. Old English custom, you know.'

'Of course, of course.' He smiled at me archly as if there was something vaguely reprehensible about this old English custom, then allowed a slightly puzzled look to replace the smile. He was as phoney as they come. 'I don't remember seeing you go out.'

'Well, now,' I said reasonably, 'you can't be expected to attend to all of your guests all of the time, can you?' I gave him his own phoney smile back again, took the key and walked towards the bank of lifts. I was less than half-way there when I brought up short as a piercing scream cut through the foyer and brought instant silence, which lasted only long enough for the woman who had screamed to draw a deep breath and start in again. The source of this racket was a middle-aged, flamboyantly dressed female, a caricature of the American tourist abroad, who was standing in front of a lift, her mouth opened in a rounded 'O', her eyes like saucers. Beside her a portly character in a seer-sucker suit was trying to calm her, but he didn't look any too happy himself and gave the impression that he wouldn't have minded doing a little screaming himself.

The assistant manager rushed past me and I followed more leisurely. By the time I reached the lift the assistant manager was on his knees, bent over the sprawled-out form of the dead waiter.

'My goodness,' I said. 'Is he ill, do you think?'

'Ill? Ill?' The assistant manager glared at me. 'Look at the way his neck is. The man's dead.'

'Good God, I do believe you're right.' I stooped and peered more closely at the waiter. 'Haven't I seen this man somewhere before?

'He was your floor-waiter,' the assistant manager said, which is not an easy remark to make with your teeth clamped together.

'I thought he looked familiar. In the midst of life—' I shook my head sadly. 'Where's the restaurant?'

'Where's the—where's the—'

'Never mind,' I said soothingly, 'I can see you're upset. I'll find it myself.'

The restaurant of the Hotel Rembrandt may not be, as the owners claim, the best in Holland, but I wouldn't care to take them to court on a charge of misrepresentation. From the caviare to the fresh out-of-season strawberries—I won-

41

dered idly whether to charge this in the expense account as entertainment or bribes—the food was superb. I thought briefly, but not guiltily, about Maggie and Belinda, but such things had to be. The red plush sofa on which I was sitting was the ultimate in dining comfort, so I leaned back in it, lifted my brandy glass and said, 'Amsterdam!'

'Amsterdam!' said Colonel Van de Graaf. The Colonel, deputy head of the city's police, had joined me, without invitation, only five minutes previously. He was sitting in a large chair which seemed too small for him. A very broad man of only medium height, he had iron-grey hair, a deeply-trenched, tanned face, the unmistakable cast of authority and an air about him of almost dismaying competence. He went on dryly: 'I'm glad to see you enjoying yourself, Major Sherman, after such an eventful day.'

'Gather ye rosebuds while you may, Colonel—life is all too short. What events?'

'We have been unable to discover very much about this man, James Duclos, who was shot and killed at the airport today.' A patient man and not one to be easily drawn, was Colonel de Graaf. 'We know only that he arrived from England three weeks ago, that he checked into the Hotel Schiller for one night and then disappeared. He seems, Major Sherman, to have been meeting your plane. Was this, one asks, just coincidence?'

'He was meeting me.' De Graaf was bound to find out sooner or later. 'One of my men. I think he must have got hold of a forged police pass from somewhere—to get past immigration, I mean.'

'You surprise me.' He sighed heavily and didn't seem in the least surprised. 'My friend, it makes it very difficult for us if we don't know those things. I should have been told about Duclos. As we have instructions from Interpol in Paris to give you every possible assistance, don't you think it would be better if we can work together? We can help you—you can help us.' He sipped some brandy. His grey eyes were very direct. 'One would assume that this man of yours had information—and now we have lost it.'

'Perhaps. Well, let's start by you helping me. Can you see if you have a Miss Astrid Lemay on your files? Works in a night-club but she doesn't sound Dutch and she doesn't look Dutch so you may have something on her.'

'The girl you knocked down at the airport? How do you know she works in a night-club.'

'She told me,' I said unblushingly.

He frowned. 'The airport officials made no mention of any such remark to me.'

'The airport officials are a bunch of old women.'

'Ah!' It could have meant anything. 'This information I can obtain. Nothing more?'

'Nothing more.'

'One other little event we have not referred to.'

'Tell me.'

'The sixth-floor waiter—an unsavoury fellow about whom we know a little—was *not* one of your men?'

'Colonel!'

'I didn't for a moment think he was. Did you know that he died of a broken neck?'

'He must have had a very heavy fall,' I said sympathetically.

De Graaf drained his brandy and stood up.

'We are not acquainted with you, Major Sherman, but you have been too long in Interpol and gained too much of a European reputation for us not to be acquainted with your methods. May I remind you that what goes in Istanbul and Marseilles and Palermo—to name but a few places—does not go in Amsterdam?'

'My word,' I said. 'You *are* well informed.'

'Here, in Amsterdam, we are all subject to the law.' He might not have heard me. 'Myself included. You are no exception.'

'Nor would I expect to be,' I said virtuously. 'Well then, co-operation. The purpose of my visit. When can I talk to you?'

'My office, ten o'clock.' He looked around the restaurant without enthusiasm. 'Here is hardly the time and place.'

I raised an eyebrow.

'The Hotel Rembrandt,' said de Graaf heavily, 'is a listening-post of international renown.'

'You astonish me,' I said.

De Graaf left. I wondered why the hell he thought I'd chosen to stay in the Hotel Rembrandt.

Colonel de Graaf's office wasn't in the least like the Hotel Rembrandt. It was a large enough room, but bleak and bare and functional, furnished mainly with steel-grey filing cabinets, a steel-grey table and steel-grey seats which were as hard as steel. But at least the decor had the effect of making you concentrate on the matter on hand: there was nothing to distract the mind or eye. De Graaf and I, after ten minutes preliminary discussion, were concentrating, although I think it came more easily to de Graaf than it did to me. I had lain awake to a late hour the previous night and am never at my best at ten a.m. on a cold and blustery morning.

'All drugs,' de Graaf agreed. 'Of course we're concerned with all drugs—opium, cannabis, amphetamine, LSD, STP, cocaine, amyl acetate—you name it, Major Sherman, and we're concerned in it. They all destroy or lead on to destruction. But in this instance we are confining ourselves to the really evil one—heroin. Agreed?'

'Agreed.' The deep incisive voice came from the doorway. I turned round and looked at the man who stood there, a tall man in a well-cut dark business suit, cool penetrating grey eyes, a pleasant face that could stop being pleasant very quickly, very professional-looking. There was no mistaking his profession. Here was a cop and not one to be taken lightly either.

He closed the door and walked across to me with the light springy step of a man much younger than one in his middle forties, which he was at least. He put out his hand and said: 'Van Gelder. I've heard a lot about you, Major Sherman.'

I thought this one over, briefly but carefully, decided to refrain from comment I smiled and shook his hand.

'Inspector van Gelder,' de Graaf said. 'Head of our narcotics bureau. He will be working with you, Sherman. He will offer you the best co-operation possible.'

'I sincerely hope we can work well together.' Van Gelder smiled and sat down. 'Tell me, what progress your end? Do you think you can break the supply ring in England?'

'I think we could. It's a highly organized distributive pipeline, very highly integrated with almost no cut-offs —and it's because of that that we have been able to identify dozens of their pushers and the half-dozen or so main distributors.'

'You could break the ring but you won't. You're leaving it strictly alone?'

'What else, Inspector? We break them up and the next distribution ring will be driven so far underground that we'll never find it. As it is, we can pick them up when and if we want to. The thing we really want to find out is how the damned stuff gets in—and who's supplying it.'

'And you think—obviously, or you wouldn't be here— that the supplies come from here? Or hereabouts?'

'Not hereabouts. Here. And I don't think. I know. Eighty per cent of those under surveillance—and I refer to the distributors and their intermediaries—have links with this country. To be precise, with Amsterdam—nearly all of them. They have relatives here, or they have friends. They have business contacts here or personally conduct business here or they come here on holiday. We've spent five years on building up this dossier.'

De Graaf smiled. 'On this place called "here".'

'On Amsterdam, yes.'

Van Gelder asked: 'There are copies of this dossier?'

'One.'

'With you?'

'Yes.'

'On you?'

'In the only safe place.' I tapped my head.

'As safe a place as any,' de Graaf approved, then

added thoughtfully: 'As long, of course, that you don't meet up with people who might be inclined to treat you the way you treat them.'

'I don't understand, Colonel.'

'I speak in riddles,' de Graaf said affably. 'All right, I agree. At the moment the finger points at the Netherlands. Not to put too fine a point on it, as you don't put too fine a point on it, at Amsterdam. We, too, know our unfortunate reputation. We wish it was untrue. But it isn't. We *know* the stuff comes in in bulk. We *know* it goes out again all broken up—but from where or how we have no idea.'

'It's your bailiwick,' I said mildly.

'It's what?'

'It's your province. It's in Amsterdam. You run the law in Amsterdam.'

'Do you make many friends in the course of a year?' van Gelder enquired politely.

'I'm not in this business to make friends.'

'You're in this business to destroy people who destroy people,' de Graaf said pacifically. 'We know about you. We have a splendid dossier on you. Would you like to see it?'

'Ancient history bores me.'

'Predictably.' De Graaf sighed. 'Look, Sherman, the best police forces in the world can come up against a concrete wall. That's what we have done—not that I claim we're the best. All we require is one lead—one single solitary lead . . . Perhaps you have some idea, some plan?'

'I arrived only yesterday.' I fished inside the inside of my lower right trouser-leg and gave the Colonel the two scraps of paper I'd found in the dead floor-waiter's pockets. 'Those figures. Those numbers. They mean anything to you?'

De Graaf gave them a cursory glance, held them up before a bright desk-lamp, laid them down on the desk. 'No.'

'Can you find out? If they have any meaning?'

'I have a very able staff. By the way, where did you get these?'

'A man gave them to me.'

46

'You mean you got them from a man.'

'There's a difference?'

'There could be a very great difference,' De Graaf leaned forward, face and voice very earnest. 'Look, Major Sherman, we know about your technique of getting people off balance and keeping them there. We know about your propensity for stepping outside the law—'

'Colonel de Graaf!'

'A well-taken point. You're probably never inside it to start with. We know about this deliberate policy—admittedly as effective as it is suicidal—of endless provocation, waiting for something, for somebody to break. But please, Major Sherman, *please* do not try to provoke too many people in Amsterdam. We have too many canals.'

'I won't provoke anyone,' I said. 'I'll be very careful.'

'I'm sure you will.' De Graaf sighed. 'And now, I believe, van Gelder has a few things to show you.'

Van Gelder had. He drove me in his own black Opel from the police HQ in the Marnixstraat to the city mortuary and by the time I left there I was wishing he hadn't.

The city mortuary lacked the old-world charm, the romance and nostalgic beauty of old Amsterdam. It was like the city mortuary in any big town, cold—very cold—and clinical and inhuman and repelling. The central block had down its centre two rows of white slabs of what appeared to be marble and almost certainly wasn't, while the sides of the room were lined with very large metal doors. The principal attendant here, resplendent in an immaculately starched white coat, was a cheerful, rubicund, genial character who appeared to be in perpetual danger of breaking out into gales of laughter, a very odd characteristic indeed, one would have thought, to find in a mortuary attendant until one recalled that more than a handful of England's hangmen in the past were reckoned to be the most rollicking tavern companions one could ever hope to have.

At a word from van Gelder, he led us to one of the big metal doors, opened it and pulled out a wheeled metal rack

47

that ran smoothly on steel runners. A white-sheeted form lay on this rack.

'The canal he was found in is called the Croquiskade,' van Gelder said. He seemed quite unemotional about it. 'Not what you might call the Park Lane of Amsterdam —it's down by the docks. Hans Gerber. Nineteen. I won't show you his face—he's been too long in the water. The fire brigade found him when they were fishing out a car. He could have been there another year or two. Someone had twisted a few old lead pipes about his middle.'

He lifted a corner of the sheet to expose a flaccid emaciated arm. It looked for all the world as if someone had trodden all over it with spiked climbing boots. Curious purple lines joined many of those punctures and the whole arm was badly discoloured. Van Gelder covered it up without a word and turned away. The attendant wheeled the rack inside again, closed the door, led us to another door and repeated the performance of wheeling out another corpse, smiling hugely the while like a bankrupt English duke showing the public round his historic castle.

'I won't show you this one's face either,' van Gelder said. 'It is not nice to look on a boy of twenty-three who has the face of a man of seventy.' He turned to the attendant. 'Where was this one found?'

'The Oosterhook,' the attendant beamed. 'On a coal barge.'

Van Gelder nodded. 'That's right. With a bottle—an empty bottle—of gin beside him. The gin was all inside him. You know what a splendid combination gin and heroin is.' He pulled back the sheet to reveal an arm similar to the one I'd just seen. 'Suicide—or murder?'

'It all depends.'

'On?'

'Whether he bought the gin himself. That would make it suicide—or accidental death. Someone could have put the full bottle in his hand. That would make it murder. We had a case just like it last month in the Port of London. We'll never know.'

At a nod from van Gelder, the attendant led us happily to a slab in the middle of the room. This time van Gelder pulled back the sheet from the top. The girl was very young and very lovely and had golden hair.

'Beautiful, isn't she?' van Gelder asked. 'Not a mark on her face. Julia Rosemeyer from East Germany. All we know of her, all we will ever know of her. Sixteen, the doctors guess.'

'What happened to her?'

'Fell six stories to a concrete pavement.'

I thought briefly of the ex-floor-waiter and how much better he would have looked on this slab, then asked: 'Pushed?'

'Fell. Witnesses. They were all high. She'd been talking all night about flying to England. She had some obsession about meeting the Queen. Suddenly she scrambled on to the parapet of the balcony, said she was flying to see the Queen—and, well, she flew. Fortunately, there was no one passing beneath at the time. Like to see more?'

'I'd like to have a drink at the nearest pub, if you don't mind.'

'No.' He smiled but there wasn't anything humorous about it. 'Van Gelder's fireside. It's not far. I have my reasons.'

'Your reasons?'

'You'll see.'

We said goodbye and thanks to the happily smiling attendant, who looked as if he would have liked to say, 'Haste ye back' but didn't. The sky had darkened since early morning and big heavy scattered drops of rain were beginning to fall. To the east the horizon was livid and purple, more than vaguely threatening and foreboding. It was seldom that a sky reflected my mood as accurately as this.

Van Gelder's fireside could have given points to most English pubs I knew: an oasis of bright cheerfulness compared to the sheeting rain outside, to the rippled waves of water running down the windows, it was warm and cosy and comfortable and homely, furnished in rather heavy Dutch furniture with over-stuffed armchairs, but I have a strong partiality for over-stuffed armchairs: they don't mark you so much as the understuffed variety. There was a russet carpet on the floor and the walls were painted in different shades of warm pastel colours. The fire was all a fire ever should be and van Gelder, I was happy to observe, was thoughtfully studying a very well-stocked glass liquor cupboard.

'Well,' I said, 'you took me to that damned mortuary to make your point. I'm sure you made it. What was it?'

'Points, not point. The first one was to convince you that we here are up against an even more vicious problem than you have at home. There's another half-dozen drug addicts in the mortuary there and how many of them died a natural death is anyone's guess. It's not always as bad as this, those deaths seem to come in waves, but it still represents an intolerable loss of life and mainly young life at that: and for every one there, how many hundred hopeless addicts are there in the streets?'

'Your point being that you have even more incentive than I to seek out and destroy those people—and that we are attacking a common enemy, a central source of supply?'

'Every country has only one king.'

'And the other point?'

'To reinforce Colonel de Graaf's warning. Those people are totally ruthless. Provoke them too much, get too close to them—well, there's still a few slabs left in the mortuary.'

'How about that drink?' I said.

A telephone bell rang in the hallway outside. Van Gelder murmured an apology and went to answer it. Just as the door closed behind him a second door leading to the room opened and a girl entered. She was tall and slender and in her early twenties and was dressed in a dragon-emblazoned multi-hued housecoat that reached almost to her ankles. She was quite beautiful, with flaxen hair, an oval face and huge violet eyes that appeared to be at once humorous and perceptive, so striking in overall appearance that it was quite some time before I remembered what passed for my manners and struggled to my feet, no easy feat from the depths of that cavernous armchair.

'Hullo,' I said. 'Paul Sherman.' It didn't sound much but I couldn't think of anything else to say.

Almost as if embarrassed, the girl momentarily sucked the tip of her thumb, then smiled to reveal perfect teeth.

'I am Trudi. I do not speak good English.' She didn't either, but she'd the nicest voice for speaking bad English I'd come across in a long time. I advanced with my hand out, but she made no move to take it: instead she put her hand to her mouth and giggled shyly. I am not accustomed to have fully-grown girls giggle shyly at me and was more than a little relieved to hear the sound of the receiver being replaced and van Gelder's voice as he entered from the hall.

'Just a routine report on the airport business. Nothing to go on yet—'

Van Gelder saw the girl, broke off, smiled and advanced to put his arm round her shoulders.

'I see you two have met each other.'

'Well,' I said, 'not quite—' then broke off in turn as Trudi reached up and whispered in his ear, glancing at me out of the corner of her eye. Van Gelder smiled and nodded and Trudi went quickly from the room. The puzzlement must have shown in my face, for van Gelder smiled again and it didn't seem a very happy smile to me.

'She'll be right back, Major. She's shy at first, with strangers. Just at first.'

As van Gelder had promised, Trudi was back almost immediately. She was carrying with her a very large puppet, so wonderfully made that at first glance it could have been mistaken for a real child. It was almost three feet in length with a white wimple hat covering flaxen curls of the same shade as Trudi's own and was wearing an ankle-length billowy striped silk dress and a most beautifully embroidered bodice. Trudi clasped this puppet as tightly as if it had been a real child. Van Gelder again put his arm round her shoulders.

51

'This is my daughter, Trudi. A friend of mine, Trudi. Major Sherman, from England.'

This time she advanced without any hesitation, put her hand out, made a small bobbing motion like the beginnings of a curtsy, and smiled.

'How do you do, Major Sherman?'

Not to be outdone in courtesy I smiled and bowed slightly. 'Miss van Gelder. My pleasure.'

'My pleasure.' She turned and looked enquiringly at van Gelder.

'English is not one of Trudi's strong points,' van Gelder said apologetically. 'Sit down, Major, sit down.'

He took a bottle of Scotch from the sideboard poured drinks for myself and himself, handed me mine and sank into his chair with a sigh. Then he looked up at his daughter, who was gazing steadily at me in a way that made me feel more than vaguely uncomfortable.

'Won't you sit down, my dear?'

She turned to van Gelder, smiled brightly, nodded and handed the huge puppet to him. He accepted it so readily that he was obviously used to this sort of thing.

'Yes, Papa,' she said, then without warning but at the same time as unaffectedly as if it were the most natural thing in the world, she sat down on my knee, put an arm around my neck and smiled at me. I smiled right back, though, for just that instant, it was a Herculean effort.

Trudi regarded me solemnly and said: 'I like you.'

'And I like you too, Trudi.' I squeezed her shoulder to show her how much I liked her. She smiled at me, put her head on my shoulder and closed her eyes. I looked at the top of the blonde head for a moment, then glanced in mild enquiry at van Gelder. He smiled, a smile full of sorrow.

'If I do not wound you, Major Sherman, Trudi loves everyone.'

'All girls of a certain age do.'

'You are a man of quite extraordinary perception.'

I didn't think it called for any great perception at all to

make the remark I had just made, so I didn't answer, just smiled and turned again to Trudi. I said, very gently: 'Trudi?'

She said nothing. She just stirred and smiled again, a curiously contented smile that for some obscure reason made me feel more than a little of a fraud, closed her eyes even more tightly and snuggled close to me.

I tried again. 'Trudi. I'm sure you must have beautiful eyes. Can I see them?'

She thought this over for a bit, smiled again, sat up, held herself at straight arm's length with her hands on my shoulders, then opened her eyes very wide as a child would do on such a request.

The huge violet eyes were beautiful, no doubt about that. But they were something else also. They were glazed and vacant and did not seem to reflect the light: they sparkled, a sparkle that would have deceptively highlit any still photograph taken of her, for the sparkle was superficial only: behind lay a strange quality of opacity.

Still gently, I took her right hand from my shoulder and pushed the sleeve up as far as the elbow. If the rest of her were anything to go by it should have been a beautiful forearm but it wasn't: it was shockingly mutilated by the punctures left by a countless number of hypodermic needles. Trudi, her lips trembling, looked at me in dismay as if fearful of reproach, snatched down the sleeve of her dress, flung her arms about me, buried her face in my neck and started to cry. She cried as if her heart was breaking. I patted her as soothingly as one can pat anyone who seems bent on choking you and looked over at van Gelder.

'Now I know your reasons,' I said. 'For insisting I come here.'

'I'm sorry. Now you know.'

'You make a third point?'

'I make a third point. God alone knows I wish I didn't have to. But you will understand that in all fairness to my colleagues I must let them know these things.'

'De Graaf knows?'

'Every senior police officer in Amsterdam knows,' van Gelder said simply. 'Trudi!'

Trudi's only reaction was to cling even more tightly. I was beginning to suffer from anoxia.

'Trudi!' Van Gelder was more insistent this time. 'Your afternoon's sleep. You know what the doctor says. Bed!'

'No,' she sobbed. 'No bed.'

Van Gelder sighed and raised his voice: 'Herta!'

Almost as if she had been waiting for her cue—which she probably had been, listening outside the door—a most outlandish creature entered the room. As far as health farms were concerned, she was the challenge to end all challenges. She was a huge and enormously fat waddling woman—to describe her method of locomotion as walking would have been a gross inaccuracy—dressed in exactly the same type of clothes as Trudi's puppet was wearing. Long blonde pigtails tied with bright ribbon hung down her massive front. Her face was old—she had to be at least over seventy—deeply trenched and had the texture and appearance of cracked brown leather. The contrast between the gaily hued clothes and the blonde pigtails on the one hand and the enormous old hag that wore them on the other, was bizarre, horrible, so grotesque as to be almost obscene, but the contrast appeared to evoke no such responses in either van Gelder or Trudi.

The old woman crossed the room—for all her bulk and waddling gait she made ground quite quickly—nodded a curt acknowledgment to me and, without saying a word, laid a kindly but firm hand on Trudi's shoulder. Trudi looked up at once, her tears gone as quickly as they had come, smiled, nodded docilely, disengaged her arms from my neck and rose. She crossed to van Gelder's chair, recovered her puppet, kissed him, crossed to where I was sitting, kissed me as unaffectedly as a child saying good night, and almost skipped from the room, the waddling Herta close behind. I exhaled a long sigh and just managed to refrain from mopping my brow.

'You might have warned me,' I complained. 'About

Trudi *and* Herta. Who is she anyway—Herta, I mean? A nurse?'

'An ancient retainer, you'd say in English.' Van Gelder took a large gulp of his whisky as if he needed it and I did the same for I needed it even more: after all he was used to this sort of thing. 'My parents' old housekeeper—from the island of Huyler in the Zuider Zee. As you may have noticed, they are a little—what do you say—conservative in their dress. She's been with us for only a few months —but, well, you can see how she is with Trudi.'

'And Trudi?'

'Trudi is eight years old. She has been eight years old for the past fifteen years, she always will be eight years old. Not my daughter, as you may have guessed—but I could never love a daughter more. My brother's adopted daughter. He and I worked in Curaçao until last year—I was in narcotics, he was the security officer for a Dutch oil company. His wife died some years ago—and then he and *my* wife were killed in a car crash last year. Someone had to take Trudi. I did. I didn't want her—and now I couldn't live without her. She will never grow up, Mr Sherman.'

And all the time his subordinates probably thought that he was just their lucky superior with no other thought or concern in his mind than to put as many malefactors behind bars as possible. Sympathetic comment and commiseration were never my forte, so I said: 'This addiction—when did it start?'

'God knows. Years ago. Years before my brother found out.'

'Some of those hypo punctures are recent.'

'She's on withdrawal treatment. Too many injections, you would say?'

'I would say.'

'Herta watches her like a hawk. Every morning she takes her to the Vondel Park—she loves to feed the birds. In the afternoon Trudi sleeps. But sometimes in the evening Herta gets tired—and I am often from home in the evening.'

55

You've had her watched?'

'A score of times. I don't know how it's done.'

'They get at her to get at you?'

'To bring pressure to bear on me. What else? She has no money to pay for fixes. They are fools and do not realize that I must see her die slowly before my eyes before I can compromise myself. So they keep trying.'

'You could have a twenty-four-hour guard placed on her.'

'And then that would make it official. Such an official request is brought to the automatic notice of the health authorities. And then?'

'An institution,' I nodded. 'For the mentally retarded. And she'd never come out again.'

'She'd never come out again.'

I didn't know what to say except goodbye, so I did that and left.

CHAPTER FOUR

I spent the afternoon in my hotel room going over the carefully documented and cross-indexed files and case histories which Colonel de Graaf's office had given me. They covered every known case of drug-taking and drug prosecutions, successful or not, in Amsterdam in the past two years. They made very interesting reading if, that is, your interest lay in death and degradation and suicide and broken homes and ruined careers. But there was nothing in it for me. I spent a useless hour trying to rearrange and reassemble the various cross-indexes but no significant pattern even began to emerge. I gave up. Highly trained minds like de Graaf's and van Gelder's would have spent many, many hours in the same fruitless pastime, and if they had failed to establish any form of pattern there was no hope for me.

In the early evening I went down to the foyer and handed in my key. The smile of the assistant manager behind the desk lacked a little of the sabre-toothed quality of old, it was deferential, even apologetic: he'd obviously been told to try a new tack with me.

'Good evening, good evening, Mr Sherman.' An affable ingratiation that I cared for even less than his normal approach. 'I'm afraid I must have sounded a little abrupt last evening, but you see—'

'Don't mention it, my dear fellow, don't mention it.' I wasn't going to let any old hotel manager outdo me in affability. 'It was perfectly understandable in the circumstances. Must have come as a very great shock to you.' I glanced through the foyer doors at the falling rain. 'The guide-books didn't mention this.'

He smiled widely as if he hadn't heard the same inane remark a thousand times before, then said cunningly: 'Hardly the night for your English constitutional, Mr Sherman.'

'No chance anyway. It's Zaandam for me tonight.'

'Zaandam.' He made a face. 'My commiserations, Mr Sherman.' He evidently knew a great deal more about Zaandam than I did, which was hardly surprising as I'd just picked the name from a map.

I went outside. Rain or no rain, the barrel-organ was still grinding and screeching away at the top of its form. It was Puccini who was on the air tonight and he was taking a terrible beating. I crossed to the organ and stood there for some time, not so much listening to the music, for there was none to speak of, but looking without seeming to look at a handful of emaciated and ill-dressed teen-agers—a rare sight indeed in Amsterdam where they don't go in for emaciation very much—who leaned their elbows on the barrel-organ and seemed lost in rapture. My thoughts were interrupted by a gravelly voice behind me.

'Mynheer likes music?' I turned. The ancient was smiling at me in a tentative sort of fashion.

'I love music.'

'So do I, so do I.' I peered at him closely, for in the nature of things his time must be close and there could be no forgiveness for that remark. I smiled at him, one music-lover to the other.

'I shall think of you tonight. I'm going to the opera.'

'Mynheer is kind.'

I dropped two coins in the tin can that had mysteriously appeared under my nose.

'Mynheer is too kind.'

Having the suspicions I did about him, I thought the same myself, but I smiled charitably and, recrossing the street, nodded to the doorman: with the masonic legerdemain known only to doormen, he materialized a taxi out of nowhere. I told him 'Schiphol Airport' and got inside.

We moved off. We did not move off alone. At the first traffic lights, twenty yards from the hotel, I glanced through the tinted rear window. A yellow-striped Mercedes taxi was two cars behind us, a taxi I recognized as one that habitually frequented the rank not far from the hotel. But it could have been coincidence. The lights turned to green and we made our way into the Vijzelstraat. So did the yellow-striped Mercedes.

I tapped the driver on the shoulder. 'Stop here, please. I want to buy some cigarettes.' I got out. The Mercedes was right behind us, stopped. No one got in, no one got out. I went into an hotel foyer, bought some cigarettes I didn't need and came out again. The Mercedes was still there. We moved off and after a few moments I said to the driver: 'Turn right along the Prinsengracht.'

He protested. 'That is not the way to Schiphol.'

'It's the way I want to go. Turn right.'

He did and so did the Mercedes.

'Stop.' He stopped. The Mercedes stopped. Coincidence was coincidence but this was ridiculous. I got out, walked back to the Mercedes and opened the door. The driver was a small man with a shiny blue suit and a disreputable air. 'Good evening. Are you for hire?'

'No.' He looked me up and down, trying out first the air of easy insouciance, then that of insolent indifference, but he wasn't right for either part.

'Then why are you stopped?'

'Any law against a man stopping for a smoke?'

'None. Only you're not smoking. You know the Police HQ in the Marnixstraat?' The sudden lack of enthusiasm in his expression made it quite clear that he knew it all too well. 'I suggest you go there and ask for either Colonel de Graaf or Inspector van Gelder and tell them that you have a complaint to lodge about Paul Sherman, Room 616, Hotel Excelsior.'

'Complaint?' he said warily. 'What complaint?'

'Tell them that he took the car keys from your ignition and threw them into the canal.' I took the car keys from the ignition and threw them into the canal and a very satisfactory plop they made too as they vanished for ever into the depths of the Prinsengracht. 'Don't follow me around,' I said and closed the door in a manner befitting the end of our brief interview, but Mercedes are well made cars and the door didn't fall off.

Back in my own taxi I waited till we were back on the main road again, then stopped the taxi. 'I've decided to walk,' I said and paid what was owing.

'What! To Schiphol?'

I gave him the sort of tolerant smile one might expect to receive from a long-distance walker whose prowess has been called in question, waited till he had moved from sight, hopped on a 16 tram and got off at the Dam. Belinda, dressed in a dark coat and with a dark scarf over her blonde hair, was waiting for me in the tram shelter. She looked damp and cold.

'You're late,' she said accusingly.

'Never criticize your boss, even by implication. The managerial classes always have things to attend to.'

We crossed the square, retracing the steps the grey man and I had taken the previous night, down the alley by the Krasnapolsky and along the tree-lined Oudezijds Voorburgwal, an area that is one of the cultural highlights of Amsterdam, but Belinda seemed in no mood for culture. A mercurial girl, she seemed withdrawn and remote that night, and the silence was hardly companionable. Belinda had something on her mind and if I were beginning to become any judge of Belinda my guess was that she would let me know about it sooner rather than later. I was right.

She said abruptly: 'We don't really exist for you, do we?'

'Who doesn't exist?'

'Me, Maggie, all the people who work for you. We're just ciphers.'

'Well, you know how it is,' I said pacifically. 'Ship's captain never mingles socially with the crew.'

'That's what I mean. That's what I say—we don't really exist for you. We're just puppets to be manipulated so that the master puppeteer can achieve certain ends. Any other puppets would do as well.'

I said mildly: 'We're here to do very nasty and unpleasant jobs and achieving that end is all that matters. Personalities don't enter into it. You forget that I am your boss, Belinda. I really don't think that you should be talking to me like that.'

'I'll talk to you any way I like.' Not only mercurial but a girl of spirit; Maggie would never have dreamed of talking to me like that. She considered her last remark, then said more quietly: 'I'm sorry. I shouldn't have spoken like that. But do you have to treat us in this—this detached and remote fashion and never make contact with us? We *are* people, you know—but not for you. You'd pass me in the street tomorrow and not recognize me. You don't *notice* us.'

'Oh, I notice all right. Take yourself, for instance.' I carefully refrained from looking at her as we walked along although I knew she was observing me pretty closely. 'New girl to Narcotics. Limited experience Deuxième Bureau, Paris. Dressed in navy coat, navy scarf spotted with little white edelweiss, knitted white knee-stockings, sensible flat-heeled navy shoes, buckled, five feet four, a figure, to quote a famous American writer, to make a bishop kick a hole through a stained-glass window, a quite beautiful face, platinum blonde hair that looks like spun silk when the sun shines through it, black eyebrows, green eyes, perceptive and, best of all, beginning to worry about her boss, especially his lack of humanity. Oh, I forgot. Cracked finger-nail polish, third finger, left hand, and a devastating smile enhanced—if, that is to say, that's possible—by a slightly crooked left upper eye-tooth.'

'Wow!' She was at a momentary loss for words, which I was beginning to guess was not at all in character. She glanced at the finger-nail in question and the polish was cracked, then turned to me with a smile that was just as devastating as I'd said it was. 'Maybe you do at that.'

'Do at what?'

'Care about us.'

'Of course I care.' She was beginning to confuse me with Sir Galahad and that could be a bad thing. 'All my operatives, Category Grade 1, young, female, good-looking, are like daughters to me.'

61

There was a long pause, then she murmured something, very *sotto voce* indeed, but it sounded to me very like 'Yes, Papa.'

'What was that?' I asked suspiciously.

'Nothing. Nothing at all.'

We turned into the street which housed the premises of Morgenstern and Muggenthaler. This, my second visit to the place, more than confirmed the impression I had formed the previous night. It seemed darker than ever, bleaker and more menacing, cobbles and pavement more cracked than before, the gutters more choked with litter. Even the gabled houses leaned closer towards one another: this time tomorrow and they would be touching.

Belinda stopped abruptly and clutched my right arm. I glanced at her. She was staring upwards, her eyes wide, and I followed her gaze where the gabled warehouses marched away into the diminishing distance, their hoisting beams clearly silhouetted against the night sky. I knew she felt there was evil abroad: I felt it myself.

'This must be the place,' she whispered. 'I *know* it must be.'

'This is the place,' I said matter-of-factly. 'What's wrong?'

She snatched her hand away as if I had just said something wounding, but I regained it, tucked her arm under mine and held on firmly to her hand. She made no attempt to remove it.

'It's—it's so *creepy*. What are those horrible things sticking out under the gables?'

'Hoisting beams. In the old days the houses here were rated on the width of the frontage, so the thrifty Dutch made their houses uncommonly narrow. Unfortunately, this made their staircases even narrower still. So, the hoisting beams for the bulky stuff—grand pianos up, coffins down, that sort of thing.'

'Stop it!' She lifted her shoulders and shuddered involuntarily. 'This is a horrible place. Those beams—they're like the gallows they hang people from. This is a place where people come to die.'

'Nonsense, my dear girl,' I said heartily. I could feel stiletto-tipped fingers of ice play Chopin's Death March up and down my spine and was suddenly filled with longing for that dear old nostalgic music from the barrel-organ outside the Rembrandt: I was probably as glad to hang on to Belinda's hand as she was to mine. 'You mustn't fall prey to those Gallic imaginings of yours.'

'I'm not imagining things,' she said sombrely, then shivered again. 'Did we have to come to this awful place?' She was shivering violently now, violently and continuously, and though it was cold it wasn't as cold as all that.

'Can you remember the way we came?' I asked. She nodded, puzzled and I went on: 'You make your way back to the hotel and I'll join you later.'

'Back to the hotel?' She was still puzzled.

'I'll be all right. Now, off you go.'

She tore her hand free from mine and before I could realize what was happening she was gripping both my lapels in her hands and giving me a look that was clearly designed to shrivel me on the spot. If she was shaking now it was with anger: I'd never realized that so beautiful a girl could look so furious. 'Mercurial' was no word for Belinda, just a pale and innocuous substitute for the one I really wanted. I looked down at the fists gripping my lapels. The knuckles were white. She was actually trying to shake me.

'Don't ever say anything like that to me again.' She *was* furious, no doubt about it.

There was a brief but spirited conflict between my ingrained instinct for discipline and the desire to put my arms round her: discipline won, but it was a close run thing. I said humbly: 'I'll never say anything like that to you again.'

'All right.' She released my sadly crushed lapels and grabbed my hand instead. 'Well, come on, then.' Pride would never let me say that she dragged me along but to the detached onlooker it must have seemed uncommonly like it.

Fifty paces further along and I stopped. 'Here we are.'

Belinda read the nameplate: 'Morgenstern and Muggenthaler.'

'Topping the bill at this week's Palladium.' I climbed the steps and got to work on the lock. 'Watch the street.'

'And then what do I do?'

'Watch my back.'

A determined wolf-cub with a bent hairpin would have found that lock no deterrent. We went inside and I closed the door behind us. The torch I had was small but powerful: it didn't have much to show us on that first floor. It was piled almost ceiling high with empty wooden boxes, paper, cardboard, bales of straw and baling and binding machinery. A packing station, nothing else.

We climbed up the narrow winding wooden steps to the next floor. Half-way up I glanced round and saw that Belinda, too, was glancing apprehensively behind her, her torch swivelling and darting in a dozen different directions.

The next floor was given over entirely to vast quantities of Dutch pewter, windmills, dogs, pipes and a dozen other articles associated solely with the tourist souvenir trade. There were tens of thousands of those articles, on shelves along the walls or on parallel racks across the warehouse, and although I couldn't possibly examine them all, they all looked perfectly innocuous to me. What didn't look quite so innocuous, however, was a fifteen by twenty room that projected from one corner of the warehouse, or, more precisely, the door that led into that room, although obviously it wasn't going to lead into that room tonight. I called Belinda over and shone my torch on the door. She stared at it, then stared at me and I could see the puzzlement in the reflected wash of light.

'A time-lock,' she said. 'Why would anyone want a time-lock on a simple office door?'

'It's not a simple office door,' I pointed out. 'It's made of steel. By the same token you can bet those simple wooden walls are lined with steel and that the simple old rustic window overlooking the street is covered with close-meshed bars set in concrete. In a diamond warehouse, yes, you could understand it. But here? Why, they've nothing to hide here.'

'It looks as if we may have come to the right place,' Belinda said.

'Did you ever doubt me?'

'No, sir.' Very demure. 'What *is* this place, anyway?'

'It's obvious, isn't it—a wholesaler in the souvenir trade. The factories or the cottage industries or whatever send their goods in bulk for storage here and the warehouse supplies the shops on demand. Simple, isn't it? Harmless, isn't it?'

'But not very hygienic.'

'How's that again?'

'It smells horrible.'

'Cannabis does to some people.'

'Cannabis!'

'You and your sheltered life. Come on.'

I led the way up to the third floor, waited for Belinda to join me. 'Still guarding the master's back?' I enquired.

'Still guarding the master's back,' she said mechanically. True to form, the fire-breathing Belinda of a few minutes ago had disappeared. I didn't blame her. There was something inexplicably sinister and malevolent about this old building. The sickly smell of cannabis was even stronger now but there appeared to be nothing on this floor even remotely connected with it. Three sides of the entire floor, together with a number of transverse racks, were given over entirely to pendulum clocks, all of them, fortunately, stopped. They covered the whole gamut of shape, design and size and varied in quality from small, cheap, garishly-painted models for the tourist trade, nearly all made from yellow pine, to very large, beautifully made and exquisitely designed metal clocks that were obviously very old and expensive, or modern replicas of those, which couldn't have been all that much cheaper.

The fourth side of the floor came, to say the least, as a considerable surprise. It was given up to, of all things, row upon row of Bibles. I wondered briefly what on earth Bibles were doing in a souvenir warehouse, but only briefly: there were too many things I didn't understand.

I picked one of them up and examined it. Embossed in gold on the lower half of the leather cover were the words *The Gabriel Bible*. . . . I opened it and on the fly-leaf was the printed inscription: 'With the Compliments of the First Reformed Church of the American Huguenot Society.'

'There's one of those in our hotel room,' Belinda said.

'I shouldn't be surprised if there's one of those in most of the hotel rooms in the city. Question is, what are they doing here? Why not in a publisher's or stationer's ware-house, where you would expect to find them? Queer, isn't it?'

She shivered. 'Everything here is queer.'

I clapped her on the back. 'You've got a cold coming on, that's what it is. I've warned you before about these mini-skirts. Next floor.'

The next floor was given over entirely to the most astonishing collection of puppets imaginable. Altogether, their number must have run into thousands. They ranged in size from tiny miniatures to models even bigger than the one Trudi had been carrying: all, without exception, were exquisitely modelled, all beautifully dressed in a variety of traditional Dutch costumes. The bigger puppets were either free-standing or supported by a metal stay: the smaller ones dangled by strings from overhead rails. The beam of my torch finally focused on a group of dolls all dressed in the same particular costume.

Belinda had forgotten about the importance of minding my back: she'd resumed her arm-clutching again.

'It's—it's so eerie. They're so alive, so watchful.' She looked at the dolls spot-lit by the beam of my torch. 'Something special about those?'

'There's no need to whisper. They may be looking at you but I assure you they can't hear you. Those puppets there. Nothing special really, just that they come from the island of Huyler out in the Zuider Zee. Van Gelder's housekeeper, a charming old beldam who's lost her broomstick, dresses like that.'

'Like that?'

'It's hard to imagine,' I admitted. 'And Trudi has a big puppet dressed in exactly the same way.'

'The sick girl?'

'The sick girl.'

'There's something terribly sick about this place.' She let go of my arm and got back to the business of minding my back again. Seconds later I heard the sound of her sharply indrawn breath and turned round. She had her back to me, not more than four feet away, and as I watched she started to walk slowly and silently backwards, her eyes evidently lined up on something caught in the beam of her torch, her free hand reaching out gropingly behind her. I took it and she came close to me, still not turning her head.

She spoke in an urgent whisper.

'There's somebody there. Somebody watching.'

I glanced briefly along the beam of her torch but could see nothing, but then hers wasn't a very powerful torch compared to the one I carried. I looked away, squeezed her hand to attract her attention, and when she turned round I looked questioningly at her.

'There *is* someone there.' Still the same insistent whisper, the green eyes wide. 'I saw them. I *saw* them.'

'Them?'

'Eyes. I saw them!'

I never doubted her. Imaginative girl she might be, but she'd been trained and highly trained not to be imaginative in the matter of observation. I brought up my own torch, not as carefully as I might have done, for the beam struck her eyes in passing, momentarily blinding her and as she raised a reflex hand to her eyes I settled the beam on the area she just indicated. I couldn't see any eyes, but what I did see was two adjacent puppets swinging so gently that their motion was almost imperceptible. Almost, but not quite—and there wasn't a draught, a breath of air, stirring in that fourth floor of the warehouse.

I squeezed her hand again and smiled at her. 'Now, Belinda—'

'Don't you "now Belinda" me!' Whether this was meant to be a hiss or a whisper with a tremor in it I couldn't be sure. 'I *saw* them. Horrible staring eyes. I swear I saw them. I swear it.'

'Yes, yes, of course, Belinda—'

She moved to face me, frustration in the intent eyes as if she suspected me of sounding as if I were trying to humour her, which I was. I said, 'I believe you, Belinda. Of *course* I believe you.' I hadn't changed my tone.

'Then why don't you do something about it?'

'Just what I'm going to do. I'm going to get the hell out of here.' I made a last unhurried inspection with my torch, as if nothing had happened, then turned and took her arm in a protective fashion. 'Nothing for us here—and we've both been too long in here. A drink, I think, for what's left of our nerves.'

She stared at me, her face reflecting a changing pattern of anger and frustration and incredulity and, I suspected, more than a little relief. But the anger was dominant now: most people become angry when they feel they are being disbelieved and humoured at the same time.

'But I tell you—'

'Ah—ah!' I touched my lips with my forefinger. 'You don't tell me anything. The boss, remember, always knows best. . . .'

She was too young to go all puce and apoplectic, but the precipitating emotions were there all the same. She glared at me, apparently decided that there were no words to meet the situation, and started off down the stairs, outrage in every stiff line of her back. I followed and my back wasn't quite normal either, it had a curious tingling feeling to it that didn't go away until I had the front door to the warehouse safely locked behind me.

We walked quickly up the street, keeping about three feet apart: it was Belinda who maintained the distance, her attitude clearly proclaiming that the hand-holding and the arm-clutching was over for the night and more likely for keeps. I cleared my throat.

'He who fights and runs away, lives to fight another day.'

She was so seething with anger that she didn't get it.

'Please don't talk to me,' she snapped so I didn't, not, at least, till I came to the first tavern in the sailors' quarter, an unsalubrious dive rejoicing in the name of 'The Cat o' Nine Tails'. The British Navy must have stopped by here once. I took Belinda's arm and guided her inside. She wasn't keen, but she didn't fight about it.

It was a smoky airless drinking den and that was about all you could say about it. Several sailors, resentful of this intrusion by a couple of trippers of what they probably rightly regarded as their own personal property, scowled at me when I came in, but I was in a much better scowling mood than they were and after the first disparaging reception they left us strictly alone. I led Belinda to a small table, a genuine antique wooden table whose original surface hadn't been touched by soap or water since time immemorial.

'I'm having Scotch,' I said. 'You?'

'Scotch,' she said huffily.

'But you don't drink Scotch.'

'I do tonight.'

She was half right. She knocked back half of her glass of neat Scotch in a defiant swig and then started spluttering, coughing and choking so violently that I saw I could have been wrong about her developing symptoms of apoplexy. I patted her helpfully on the back.

'Take your hand away,' she wheezed.

I took my hand away.

'I don't think I can work with you any more, Major Sherman,' she said after she'd got her larynx in working order again.

'I'm sorry to hear that.'

'I can't work with people who don't trust me, who don't believe me. You not only treat us like puppets, you treat us like children.'

'I don't regard you as a child,' I said pacifically. I didn't either.

' "I believe you, Belinda",' she mimicked bitterly. ' "Of course I believe you, Belinda". You don't believe Belinda at all.'

'I *do* believe Belinda,' I said. 'I do believe I care for Belinda after all. That's why I took Belinda out of there.'

She stared at me. 'You believe—then why—'

'There *was* someone there, hidden behind that rack of puppets. I saw two of the puppets sway slightly. Someone was behind the rack, watching, waiting to see, I'm certain, what, if anything, we found out. He'd no murderous intent or he'd have shot us in the back when we were going down the stairs. But if I'd reacted as you wanted me to, then I'd have been forced to go look for him and he'd have gunned me down from his place of concealment before I'd even set eyes on him. And then he'd have gunned you down, for he couldn't have any witnesses, and you're really far too young to die yet. Or maybe I could have played hide-and-seek with him and stood an even chance of getting him—if you weren't there. But you were, you haven't a gun, you've no experience at all in the nasty kind of games we play and you were as good as a hostage to him. So I took Belinda out of there. There now, wasn't that a nice speech?'

'I don't know about the speech.' Mercurial as ever, there were tears in her eyes. 'I only know it's the nicest thing anybody ever said about me.'

'Fiddlesticks!' I drained my Scotch, finished hers off for her and took her back to her hotel. We stood in the foyer entrance for a moment, sheltering from the now heavily falling rain and she said: 'I'm sorry. I was such a fool. And I'm sorry for you too.'

'For me?'

'I can see now why you'd rather have puppets than people working for you. One doesn't cry inside when a puppet dies.'

I said nothing. I was beginning to lose my grip on this

girl, the old master-pupil relationship wasn't quite what it used to be.

'Another thing,' she said. She spoke almost happily.

I braced myself.

'I won't ever be afraid of you any more.'

'You were afraid? Of me?'

'Yes, I was. Really. But it's like the man said—'

'What man?'

'Shylock, wasn't it. You know, cut me and I bleed—'

'Oh, do be quiet!'

She kept quiet. She just gave me that devastating smile again, kissed me without any great haste, gave me some more of the same smile and went inside. I watched the glass swing-doors until they came to a rest. Much more of this, I thought gloomily, and discipline would be gone to hell and back again.

CHAPTER FIVE

I walked two or three hundred yards till I was well clear of the girls' hotel, picked up a taxi and was driven back to the Rembrandt. I stood for a moment under the foyer canopy, looking at the barrel-organ across the road. The ancient was not only indefatigable but apparently also impermeable, rain meant nothing to him, nothing except an earthquake would have stopped him from giving his evening performance. Like the old trouper who feels that the show must go on, he perhaps felt he had a duty to his public, and a public he incredibly had, half a dozen youths whose threadbare clothes gave every indication of being completely sodden, a group of acolytes lost in the mystic contemplation of the death agonies of Strauss, whose turn it was to be stretched on the rack tonight. I went inside.

The assistant manager caught sight of me as I turned from hanging up my coat. His surprise appeared to be genuine.

'Back so soon? From Zaandam?'

'Fast taxi,' I explained and passed through to the bar, where I ordered a *jonge Genever* and a Pils and drank both slowly while I considered the relationship between fast men with fast guns and pushers and sick girls and hidden eyes behind puppets and people and taxis who followed me everywhere I went and policemen being blackmailed and venal managers and door-keepers and tinny barrel-organs. It all added up to nothing. I wasn't, I felt sure, being provocative enough and was coming to the reluctant conclusion that there was nothing else for it but a visit to the warehouse again later that night—without, of course, ever letting Belinda know about it—when I happened to look up for the first time at the mirror in front of me. I wasn't prompted by instinct or anything of the kind, it was

72

just that my nostrils had been almost unconsciously titillated for some time past by a perfume that I'd just identified as sandalwood, and as I am rather partial to it, I just wanted to see who was wearing it. Sheer old-fashioned nosiness.

The girl was sitting at a table directly behind me, a drink on the table before her, a paper in her hand. I could have thought that I imagined that her eyes dropped to the paper as soon as I had glanced up to the mirror, but I wasn't given to imagining things like that. She had been looking at me. She seemed young, was wearing a green coat and had a blonde mop of hair that, in the modern fashion, had every appearance of having been trimmed by a lunatic hedge-cutter. Amsterdam seemed to be full of blondes who were forced on my attention in one way or another.

I said 'The same again' to the bar-tender, placed the drinks on a table close to the bar, left them there and walked slowly towards the foyer, passed the girl like one deep lost in thought, not even looking at her, went through the front door and out into the street. Strauss had succumbed but not the ancient, who to demonstrate his catholicity of taste was now giving a ghoulish rendering of 'The bonnie, bonnie banks of Loch Lomond'. If he tried that lot on in Sauchiehall Street in Glasgow both he and his barrel-organ would be but a faded memory inside fifteen minutes. The youthful acolytes had vanished, which could have meant that they were either very anti-Scottish or very pro-Scottish indeed. In point of fact their absence, as I was to discover later, meant something else entirely: the evidence was all there before me and I missed it and because I missed it, too many people were going to die.

The ancient saw me and registered his surprise.

'Mynheer said that he—'

'He was going to the opera. And so I did.' I shook my head sadly. 'Prima-donna reaching for a high E. Heart attack.' I clapped him on the shoulder. 'No panic. I'm only going as far as the phone-box there.'

I dialled the girls' hotel. I got through to the desk

immediately and then, after a long wait, to the girls' room. Belinda sounded peevish.

'Hullo. Who is it?'

'Sherman. I want you over here at once.'

'Now?' Her voice was a wail. 'But I'm in the middle of a bath.'

'Regrettably, I can't be in two places at once. You're clean enough for the dirty work I have in hand. And Maggie.'

'But Maggie's asleep.'

'Then you'd better wake her up, hadn't you? Unless you want to carry her.' Injured silence. 'Be here at my hotel in ten minutes. Hang about outside, about twenty yards away.'

'But it's bucketing rain!' She was still at the wailing.

'Ladies of the street don't mind how damp they get. Soon there'll be a girl leaving here. Your height, your age, your figure, your hair—'

'There must be ten thousand girls in Amsterdam who—'

'Ah— But this one is beautiful. Not as beautiful as you are, of course, but beautiful. She's also wearing a green coat—to go with her green umbrella—sandalwood perfume and, on her left temple, a fairly well camouflaged bruise that I gave her yesterday afternoon.'

'A fairly well—you didn't tell us anything about assaulting girls.'

'I can't remember every irrelevant detail. Follow her. When she gets to her destination, one of you stay put, the other report back to me. No, you can't come here, you know that. I'll be at the Old Bell at the far corner of the Rembrandtplein.'

'What will you be doing there?'

'It's a pub. What do you think I'll be doing?'

The girl in the green coat was still sitting there at the same table when I returned. I went to the reception desk first, asked for and got some notepaper and took it across to the table where I'd left my drinks. The girl in green was no more than six feet away, at right angles, and so should have had an excellent view of what I was doing while herself remaining comparatively free from observation.

I took out my wallet, extracted my previous night's dinner bill, smoothed it out on the table before me and started to make notes on a piece of paper. After a few moments I threw my pen down in disgust, screwed up the paper and flung it into a convenient waste-basket. I started on another sheet of paper and appeared to reach the same unsatisfactory conclusion. I did this several times more, then screwed my eyes shut and rested my head on my hands for almost five minutes, a man, it must have seemed, lost in the deepest concentration. The fact was, that I wasn't in too much of a hurry. Ten minutes, I'd said to Belinda, but if she managed to get out of a bath, get dressed and be across here with Maggie in that time, I knew even less than I thought I did about women.

For a time I resumed the scribbling, the crumpling and the throwing away and by that time twenty minutes had elapsed. I finished the last of my drink, rose, said good night to the barman and went away. I went as far as the wine plush curtains that screened the bar from the foyer and waited, peering cautiously round the edge of the curtain. The girl in green rose to her feet, crossed to the bar, ordered herself another drink and then casually sat down in the chair I had just vacated, her back to me. She looked around, also casually, to make sure that she was unobserved, then just as casually reached down into the waste-basket and picked up the top sheet of crumpled paper. She smoothed it out on the table before her as I moved soundlessly up to her chair. I could see the side of her face now and I could see that it had gone very still. I could even read the message she had smoothed out on the table. It read: ONLY NOSY YOUNG GIRLS LOOK IN WASTEPAPER BASKETS.

'All the other papers have the same secret message,' I said. 'Good evening, Miss Lemay.'

She twisted round and looked up at me. She'd camouflaged herself pretty well to conceal the natural olive blush of her complexion, but all the paint and powder in the world was useless to conceal the blush that spread from her neck all the way up to the forehead.

'My word,' I said. 'What a charming shade of pink.'

'I am sorry. I do not speak English.'

I very gently touched the bruise and said kindly: 'Concussive amnesia. It'll pass. How's the head, Miss Lemay?'

'I'm sorry, I—'

'Do not speak English. You said that. But you understand it well enough, don't you? Especially the written word. My word, for an ageing character like myself it's refreshing to see that the young girls of today can blush so prettily. You *do* blush prettily, you know.'

She rose in confusion, twisting and crushing the papers in her hand. On the side of the ungodly she might be—and who but those on the side of the ungodly would have tried, as no question she had tried, to block my pursuit in the airport—but I couldn't hold back a twinge of pity. There was something forlorn and defenceless about her. She could have been a consummate actress, but then consummate actresses would have been earning a fortune on the stage or screen. Then, unaccountably, I thought of Belinda. Two in the one day were two too many. I was going soft in the head. I nodded at the papers.

'You may retain those, if you wish,' I said nastily

'Those.' She looked at the papers. 'I don't want to—'

'Ha! The amnesia is wearing off.'

'Please, I—'

'Your wig's slipped, Miss Lemay.'

Automatically her hands reached up and touched her hair, then she slowly lowered them to her sides and bit her lip in chagrin. There was something close to desperation in the brown eyes. Again I had the unpleasant sensation of not feeling very proud of myself.

'Please leave me,' she said, so I stepped to one side to let her pass. For a moment she looked at me and I could have sworn there was a beseeching look in her eyes and her face was puckering slightly almost as if she were about to cry, then she shook her head and hurried away. I followed more slowly, watched her run down the steps and turn in the direction of the canal. Twenty seconds later Maggie and

Belinda passed by in the same direction. Despite the umbrellas they held, they looked very wet indeed and most unhappy. Maybe they'd got there in ten minutes after all.

I went back to the bar which I'd had no intention of leaving in the first place although I'd had to convince the girl that I was. The bar-tender, a friendly soul, beamed, 'Good evening again, sir. I thought you had gone to bed.'

'I wanted to go to bed. But my taste-buds said, No, another *jonge Genever*.'

'One should always listen to one's taste-buds, sir,' the bar-tender said gravely. He handed over the little glass. 'Prost, sir!' I lifted my glass and got back to my thinking. I thought about naïveté and how unpleasant it was to be led up garden paths and whether young girls could blush to order. I thought I'd heard of certain actresses that could but wasn't sure, so I called for another Genever to jog my memory.

The next glass I lifted in my hand was of a different order altogether, a great deal heavier and containing a great deal darker liquid. It was, in fact, a pint pot of Guinness, which might seem to be a very odd thing to find in a continental tavern, as indeed it was. But not in this one, not in the Old Bell, a horse-brass-behung hostelry more English than most English hostelries could ever hope to be. It specialized in English beers—and, as my glass testified, Irish stout.

The pub was well patronized but I had managed to get a table to myself facing the door, not because I have any Wild West aversion to sitting with my back to the door but because I wanted to spot Maggie or Belinda, whichever it was, when she came in. In the event it was Maggie. She crossed to my table and sat down. She was a very bedraggled Maggie and despite scarf and umbrella her raven hair was plastered to her cheeks.

'You all right?' I asked solicitously.

'If you call all right being soaked to the skin, then yes.' It wasn't at all like my Maggie to be as waspish as this: she must be very wet indeed.

'And Belinda?'

'She'll survive too. But I think she worries too much about you.' She waited pointedly until I'd finished taking a long satisfying swig at the Guinness. 'She hopes you aren't overdoing things.'

'Belinda is a very thoughtful girl.' Belinda knew damn well what I was doing.

'Belinda's young,' Maggie said.

'Yes, Maggie.'

'And vulnerable.'

'Yes, Maggie.'

'I don't want her hurt, Paul.' This made me sit up, mentally, anyway. She never called me 'Paul' unless we were alone, and even then only when she was sufficiently lost in thought or emotion to forget about what she regarded as the proprieties. I didn't know what to make of her remark and wondered what the hell the two of them might have been talking about. I was beginning to wish I'd left the two of them at home and brought along a couple of Dobermann Pinschers instead. At least a Dobermann would have made short work of our lurking friend in Morgenstern and Muggenthaler's.

'I said—' Maggie began.

'I heard what you said.' I drank some more stout. 'You're a very dear girl, Maggie.'

She nodded, not to indicate any agreement with what I said, just to show that for some obscure reason she found this a satisfactory answer and sipped some of the sherry I'd got for her. I skated swiftly back on to thick ice.

'Now. Where is our other lady-friend that you've been following?'

'She's in church.'

'What!' I spluttered into my tankard.

'Singing hymns.'

'Good God! And Belinda?'

'She's in church, too.'

'Is *she* singing hymns?'

'I don't know. I didn't go inside.'

'Maybe Belinda shouldn't have gone in either.'

'What safer place than a church?'

'True. True.' I tried to relax but felt uneasy.

'One of us had to stay.'

'Of course.'

'Belinda said you might like to know the *name* of the church.'

'Why should I—' I stared at Maggie. 'The First Reformed Church of the American Huguenot Society?' Maggie nodded. I pushed back my chair and rose. '*Now* you tell me. Come on.'

'What? And leave all that lovely Guinness that is so good for you?'

'It's Belinda's health I'm thinking of, not mine.'

We left, and as we left it suddenly occurred to me that the name of the church had meant nothing to Maggie. It had meant nothing to Maggie because Belinda hadn't told her when she got back to the hotel and she hadn't told her because Maggie had been asleep. And I'd wondered what the hell the two of them might have been talking about. They hadn't been talking about anything. Either this was very curious or I wasn't very clever. Or both.

As usual it was raining and as we passed along the Rembrandtplein by the Hotel Schiller, Mgagie gave a well-timed shiver.

'Look,' she said. 'There's a taxi. In fact, lots of taxis.'

'I wouldn't say that there's not a taxi in Amsterdam that's not in the pay of the ungodly,' I said with feeling, 'but I wouldn't bet a nickel on it. It's not far.'

Neither was it—by taxi. By foot it was a very considerable way indeed. But I had no intention of covering the distance on foot. I led Maggie down the Thorbeckeplein, turned left, right and left again till we came out on the Amstel. Maggie said: 'You do seem to know your way around, don't you, Major Sherman?'

'I've been here before.'

'When?'

'I forget. Last year, sometime.'

'When last year?' Maggie knew or thought she knew all my movements over the past five years and Maggie could be easily piqued. She didn't like what she called ir-regularities.

'In the spring, I think it was.'

'Two months, maybe?'

'About that.'

'You spent two months in Miami last spring,' she said accusingly. 'That's what the records say.'

'You know how I get my dates mixed up.'

'No, I don't.' She paused. 'I thought you'd never seen Colonel de Graaf and van Gelder before?'

'I hadn't.'

'But—'

'I didn't want to bother them.' I stopped by a phone-box. 'A couple of calls to make. Wait here.'

'I will not!' A very heady atmosphere, was Amsterdam's. She was getting as bad as Belinda. But she had a point —the slanting rain was sheeting down very heavily now. I opened the door and let her precede me into the booth. I called a near-by cab company whose number I knew, started to dial another number.

'I didn't know you spoke Dutch,' Maggie said.

'Neither do our friends. That's why we may get an honest taxi-driver.'

'You really don't trust anyone, do you?' Maggie said admiringly.

'I trust you, Maggie.'

'No, you don't. You just don't want to burden my beautiful head with unnecessary problems.'

'That's my line,' I complained. De Graaf came on the phone. After the usual courtesies I said: 'Those scraps of paper? No luck yet? Thank you, Colonel de Graaf, I'll call back later.' I hung up.

'What scraps of paper?' Maggie asked.

'Scraps of paper I gave him.'

'Where did you get them from?'

'A chap gave them to me last night.'

Maggie gave me her old-fashioned resigned look but said nothing. After a couple of minutes a taxi came along. I gave him an address in the old city and when we got there walked with Maggie down a narrow street to one of the canals in the dock area. I stopped at the corner.

'This is it?'

'This is it,' said Maggie.

'This' was a little grey church about fifty yards away along the canal bank. It was an ancient sway-backed crumbling edifice that appeared to be maintained in the near-vertical by faith alone, for to my untrained eye it looked to be in imminent danger of toppling into the canal. It had a short square stone tower, at least five degrees off the perpendicular, topped by a tiny steeple that leaned dangerously in the other direction. The time was ripe for the First Reformed Church of the American Huguenot Society to launch a major fund-raising drive.

That some of the adjacent buildings had been in even greater danger of collapse was evidenced by the fact that a large area of building on the canal side beyond the church had already been demolished: a giant crane, with the most enormous boom I had ever seen almost lost in the darkness above, stood in the middle of this cleared lot where rebuilding had already reached the stage of the completion of the reinforced foundations.

We walked slowly along the canal side towards the church. Clearly audible now was the sound of organ music and of women singing. It sounded very pleasant and safe and homely and nostalgic, the music drifting out over the darkened waters of the canal.

'The service seems to be still in progress,' I said. 'You go in there—'

I broke off and did a double-take at a blonde girl in a belted white raincoat who was just walking by.

'Hey!' I said.

The blonde girl had it all buttoned up about what to do when accosted by strange men in a lonely street. She took one look at me and started to run. She didn't get very far. She slipped on the wet cobbles, recovered, but only made another two or three paces before I caught up with her. She struggled briefly to escape, then relaxed and flung her arms about my neck. Maggie joined us, that old puritanical look on her face again.

'A very old friend, Major Sherman?'

'Since this morning. This is Trudi. Trudi van Gelder.'

'Oh.' Maggie laid a reassuring hand on Trudi's arm but Trudi ignored her, tightened her grip around my neck and gazed admiringly into my face from a distance of about four inches.

'I like you,' Trudi announced. 'You're nice.'

'Yes, I know, you told me. Oh hell!'

'What to do?' Maggie asked.

'What to do. I've got to get her home. I've got to *take* her home. Put her in a taxi and she'd skip at the first traffic lights. A hundred to one the old battle-axe who's supposed to be guarding her has dozed off and by this time her father's probably scouring the town. He'd find it cheaper to use a ball and chain.'

I unlocked Trudi's arms, not without some difficulty, and pushed up the sleeve of her left arm. I looked first of all at her arm, then at Maggie whose eyes widened and then lips pursed as she saw the unlovely pattern left by the hypodermic needles. I pulled down the sleeve—instead of breaking into tears as she had done last time Trudi just stood there and giggled as if it were all great fun—and examined the other forearm. I pulled that sleeve down too.

'Nothing fresh,' I said.

'You mean there's nothing fresh that you can see,' Maggie said.

'What do you expect me to do? Make her stand here in this icy rain and do a strip-tease on the banks of the canal to that organ music? Wait a moment.'

'Why?'

'I want to think,' I said patiently.

So I thought, while Maggie stood there with an expression of dutiful expectation on her face and Trudi clutched my arm in a proprietorial fashion and gazed adoringly up at me. Finally, I said:

'You haven't been seen by anybody in there?'

'Not as far as I know.'

'But Belinda has, of course.'

'Of course. But not so she would be recognized again. All the people in there have their heads covered. Belinda's wearing a scarf *and* the hood of her coat *and* she's sitting in shadow—I saw that from the doorway.'

'Get her out. Wait till the service is over, then follow Astrid. And try to memorize the faces of as many as possible of those who are attending the service.'

Maggie looked doubtful. 'I'm afraid that's going to be difficult.'

'Why?'

'Well, they all look alike.'

'They all—what are they, Chinese or something?'

'Most of them are nuns, carrying Bibles and those beads at their waists, and you can't see their hair, and they have those long black clothes and those white—'

'Maggie—' I restrained myself with difficulty— 'I know what nuns look like.'

'Yes, but there's something else. They're nearly all young and good-looking—some *very* good-looking—'

'You don't have to have a face like a bus smash to be a nun. Phone your hotel and leave the number of wherever you happen to finish up. Come on, Trudi. Home.'

She went with me docilely enough, by foot first and then by taxi, where she held my hand all the time and talked a lot of bright nonsense in a very vivacious way, like a young child being taken out on an unexpected treat. At van Gelder's house I asked the taxi to wait.

Trudi was duly scolded by both van Gelder and Herta with that vehemence and severity that always cloaks profound relief, then Trudi was led off, presumably to bed. Van Gelder poured a couple of drinks with the speed of a man who feels he requires one and asked me to sit down. I declined.

'I've a taxi outside. Where can I find Colonel de Graaf at this time of night? I want to borrow a car from him, preferably a fast one.'

Van Gelder smiled. 'No questions from me, my friend.

You'll find the Colonel at his office—I know he's working late tonight.' He raised his glass. 'A thousand thanks. I was a very, very worried man.'

'You had a police alert out for her?'

'An unofficial police alert.' Van Gelder smiled again, but wryly. 'You know why. A few trusted friends—but there are nine hundred thousand people in Amsterdam.'

'Any idea why she was so far from home?'

'At least there's no mystery about that. Herta takes her there often—to the church, I mean. All the Huyler people in Amsterdam go there. It's a Huguenot church—there's one in Huyler as well, well, not so much a church, some sort of business premises they use on Sundays as a place of worship. Herta takes her there too—the two of them go out to the island often. The churches and the Vondel Park—those are the only outings the child has.'

Herta waddled into the room and van Gelder looked at her anxiously. Herta, with what might conceivably have passed for an expression of satisfaction on her leathery features, shook her head and waddled out again.

'Well, thank God for that.' Van Gelder drained his glass. 'No injections.'

'Not this time.' I drained my glass in turn, said goodbye and left.

I paid off the taxi in the Marnixstraat. Van Gelder had phoned ahead to say I was coming and Colonel de Graaf was waiting for me. If he was busy, he showed no signs of it. He was engaged in his usual occupation of overflowing the chair he was sitting in, the desk in front of him was bare, his fingers were steepled under his chin and as I entered he brought his eyes down from a leisured contemplation of infinity.

'One assumes you make progress?' he greeted me.

'One assumes wrongly, I'm afraid.'

'What? No vistas of broad highways leading to the final solution?'

'Cul-de-sacs only.'

'Something about a car, I understand from the Inspector.'

'Please.'

'May one enquire why you wish this vehicle?'

'To drive up the cul-de-sacs. But that's not really what I came to ask you about.'

'I hardly thought it was.'

'I'd like a search warrant.'

'What for?'

'To make a search,' I said patiently. 'Accompanied by a senior officer or officers, of course, to make it legal.'

'Who? Where?'

'Morgenstern and Muggenthaler. Souvenir warehouse. Down by the docks—I don't know the address.'

'I've heard of them.' De Graaf nodded. 'I know nothing against them. Do you?'

'No.'

'So what makes you so curious about them?'

'I honest to God don't know. I want to find out why I *am* so curious. I was in their place tonight—'

'They're closed at night-time, surely.'

I dangled a set of skeleton keys in front of his eyes.

'You know it's a felony to be in possession of such instruments,' de Graaf said severely.

I put the keys back in my pocket. 'What instruments?'

'A passing hallucination,' de Graaf said agreeably.

'I'm curious about why they have a time-lock on the steel door leading to their office. I'm curious about the large stocks of Bibles carried on their premises. 'I didn't mention the smell of cannabis or the lad lurking behind the puppets. 'But what I'm really interested in getting hold of is their list of suppliers.'

'A search warrant we can arrange on any pretext,' de Graaf said. 'I'll accompany you myself. Doubtless you'll explain your interest in greater detail in the morning. Now about this car. Van Gelder has an excellent suggestion. A specially-engined police car, complete with everything from two-way radio to handcuffs, but to all appearance a taxi, will be here in two minutes. Driving a taxi, you understand, poses certain problems.'

'I'll try not to make too much on the side. Have you anything else for me?'

'Also in two minutes. Your car is bringing some information from the Records Office.'

Two minutes it was and a folder was delivered to de Graaf's desk. He looked through some papers.

'Astrid Lemay. Her real name, perhaps oddly enough. Dutch father, Grecian mother. He was a vice-consul in Athens, now deceased. Whereabouts of mother unknown. Twenty-four. Nothing known against her—nothing much known for her, either. Must say the background is a bit vague. Works as a hostess in the Balinova night-club, lives in a small flat near-by. Has one known relative, brother George, aged twenty. Ah! This may interest you. George, apparently, has spent six months as Her Majesty's guest.'

'Drugs?'

'Assault and attempted robbery, very amateurish effort, it seems. He made the mistake of assaulting a plain-clothes detective. Suspected of being an addict—probably trying to get money to buy more. All we have.' He turned to another paper. 'This MOO 144 number you gave me is the radio call-sign for a Belgian coaster, the *Marianne*, due in from Bordeaux tomorrow. I have a pretty efficient staff, no?'

'Yes.'

'When does it arrive?'

'Noon. We search it?'

'You wouldn't find anything. But please don't go near it. Any ideas on the other two numbers?'

'Nothing, I'm afraid on 910020. Or on 2798.' He paused reflectively. 'Or could that be 797 twice—you know. 797797?'

'Could be anything.'

De Graaf took a telephone directory from a drawer, put it away again, picked up a phone. 'A telephone number,' he said. '797797. Find out who's listed under that number. At once, please.'

We sat in silence till the phone rang. De Graaf listened briefly, replaced the receiver.

'The Balinova night-club,' he said.

'The efficient staff has a clairvoyant boss.'

'And where does this clairvoyance lead you to?'

'The Balinova night-club.' I stood up. 'I have a rather readily identifiable face, wouldn't you say, Colonel?'

'It's not a face people forget. And those white scars. I don't think your plastic surgeon was really trying.'

'He was trying all right. To conceal his almost total ignorance of plastic surgery. Have you any brown stain in this HQ?'

'Brown stain?' He blinked at me, then smiled widely. 'Oh no, Major Sherman! Disguise! In this day and age? Sherlock Holmes has been dead these many years.'

'If I'd half the brains Sherlock had,' I said heavily. 'I wouldn't be needing any disguise.'

CHAPTER SIX

The yellow and red taxi they'd given me appeared, from the outside, to be a perfectly normal Opel, but they seemed to have managed to put an extra engine into it. They'd put a lot of extra work into it too. It had a pop-up siren, a pop-up police light and a panel at the back which fell down to illuminate a 'Stop' sign. Under the front passenger seats were ropes and first-aid kits and tear-gas canisters: in the door pockets were handcuffs with keys attached. God alone knew what they had in the boot. Nor did I care. All I wanted was a fast car, and I had one.

I pulled up in a prohibited parking area outside the Balinova night-club, right opposite where a uniformed and be-holstered policeman was standing. He nodded almost imperceptibly and walked away with measured stride. He knew a police taxi when he saw one and had no wish to explain to the indignant populace why a taxi could get away with an offence that would have automatically got them a ticket.

I got out, locked the door, and crossed the pavement to the entrance of the night-club which had above it the flickering neon sign 'Balinova' and the outlined neon figures of two hula-hula dancers, although I failed to grasp the connection between Hawaii and Indonesia. Perhaps they were meant to be Balinese dancers, but if that were so they had the wrong kind of clothes on—or off. Two large windows were set one on either side of the entrance, and these were given up to an art exhibition of sorts which gave more than a delicate indication of the nature of the cultural delights and more esoteric scholarly pursuits that were to be found within. The occasional young lady depicted as wearing ear-rings and bangles and nothing else seemed almost indecently over-dressed. Of even greater interest, however, was the coffee-coloured countenance that looked back at me from the reflection in the glass: if I hadn't known who I was, I wouldn't have recognized myself. I went inside.

The Balinova, in the best time-honoured tradition, was small, stuffy, smoky and full of some indescribable incense, the main ingredient of which seemed to be burnt rubber, which was probably designed to induce in the customers the right frame of mind for the maximum enjoyment of the entertainment being presented to them but which had, in fact, the effect of producing olfactory paralysis in the space of a few seconds. Even without the assistance of the drifting clouds of smoke the place was deliberately ill-lit, except for the garish spot-light on the stage which, as was again fairly standard, was no stage at all but merely a tiny circular dance floor in the centre of the room.

The audience was almost exclusively male, running the gamut of ages from goggle-eyed teen-agers to sprightly and beady-eyed octogenarians whose visual acuity appeared to have remained undimmed with the passing of the years. Almost all of them were well-dressed, for the better-class Amsterdam night-clubs—those which still manage to cater devotedly to the refined palates of the jaded connoisseurs of certain of the plastic arts—are not for those who are on relief. They are, in a word, not cheap and the Balinova was very, very expensive, one of the extremely few clip joints in the city. There were a few women present, but only a few. To my complete lack of surprise, Maggie and Belinda were seated at a table near the door, with some sickly-coloured drinks before them. Both of them wore aloof expressions, although Maggie's was unquestionably the more aloof of the two.

My disguise, at the moment, seemed completely superfluous. Nobody looked at me as I entered and it was quite clear that nobody even wanted to look at me, which was understandable, perhaps, in the circumstances, as the audience were almost splitting their pebble glasses in their eagerness to miss none of the aesthetic nuances or symbolic significances of the original and thought-compelling ballet performance taking place before their enraptured eyes, in which a shapely young harridan in a bubble-bath, to the accompaniment of the discordant thumpings and asthmatic wheezings of an excruciating band that would not otherwise have been tolerated in a boiler factory, endeavoured to stretch out for a bath-towel that had been craftily placed about a yard beyond her reach. The air was electric with tension as the audience tried to figure out the very limited number of alternatives that were open to the unfortunate girl. I sat down at the table beside Belinda and gave her what, in the light of my new complexion, must have been a pretty dazzling smile. Belinda moved a rapid six inches away from me, lifting her nose a couple of inches higher in the air.

'Hoity-toity,' I said. Both girls turned to stare at me and I nodded towards the stage. 'Why doesn't one of you go and help her?'

There was a long pause, then Maggie said with great restraint: 'What on earth has happened to you?'

'I am in disguise. Keep your voice down.'

'But—but I phoned the hotel only two or three minutes ago,' Belinda said.

'And don't whisper either. Colonel de Graaf put me on to this place. She came straight back here?'

They nodded.

'And hasn't gone out again?'

'Not by the front door,' Maggie said.

'You tried to memorize the faces of the nuns as they came out? As I told you to?'

'We tried,' Maggie said.

'Notice anything odd, peculiar, out of the ordinary about any of them?'

'No, nothing. Except,' Belinda added brightly, 'that they seem to have very good-looking nuns in Amsterdam.'

'So Maggie has already told me. And that's all?'

They looked at each other, hesitating, then Maggie said: 'There was something funny. We seemed to see a lot more people going into that church than came out.'

'There *were* a lot more people in that church than came out,' Belinda said. 'I was there, you know.'

'I know,' I said patiently. 'What do you mean by "a lot"?'

'Well,' Belinda said defensively, 'a good few.'

'Ha! So now we're down to a good few. You both checked, of course, that the church was empty?'

It was Maggie's turn to be defensive. 'You told us to follow Astrid Lemay. We couldn't wait.'

'Has it occurred to you that some may have remained behind for private devotions? Or that maybe you're not very good counters?'

Belinda's mouth tightened angrily but Maggie put a hand on hers.

'That's not fair, Major Sherman.' And this was Maggie talking. 'We may make mistakes, but that's not fair.' When Maggie talked like that, I listened.

'I'm sorry, Maggie. I'm sorry, Belinda. When cowards like me get worried they take it out on people who can't hit back.' They both at once gave me that sweetly sympathetic smile that would normally have had me climbing the walls, but which I found curiously affecting at that moment, maybe that brown stain had done something to my nervous system. 'God only knows I make more mistakes than you do.' I did, and I was making one of my biggest then: I should have listened more closely to what the girls were saying.

'And now?' Maggie asked.

'Yes, what do we do now?' Belinda said.

I was clearly forgiven. 'Circulate around the night-clubs hereabouts. Heaven knows there's no shortage of them. See if you can recognize anyone there—performer, staff, maybe even a member of the audience—who looks like anyone you saw in the church tonight.'

Belinda stared at me in disbelief. 'Nuns in a night-club?'

'Why not? Bishops go to garden parties, don't they?'

'It's not the same thing—'

'Entertainment is entertainment the world over,' I said pontifically. 'Especially check for those who are wearing long-sleeved dresses or those fancy elbow-length gloves.'

'Why those?' Belinda asked.

'Use your head. See—if you do find anyone—if you can find out where they live. Be back in your hotel by one o'clock. I'll see you there.'

'And what are you going to do?' Maggie asked.

I looked leisurely around the club. 'I've got a lot of research to do here yet.'

'I'll bet you have,' Belinda said.

Maggie opened her mouth to speak but Belinda was saved the inevitable lecture by the reverential 'oohs' and 'aahs' and gasps of unstinted admiration, freely given, that suddenly echoed round the club. The audience were almost out of their seats. The distressed artiste had resolved her dreadful dilemma by the simple but ingenious and highly effective expedient of tipping the tin bath over and using it, tortoise-shell fashion, to conceal her maidenly blushes as she covered the negligible distance towards the salvation of the towel. She stood up, swathed in her towel, Venus arising from the depths, and bowed with regal graciousness towards the audience, Madame Melba taking her final farewell of Covent Garden. The ecstatic audience whistled and called for more, none more so than the octogenarians, but in vain: her repertoire exhausted, she shook her head prettily and minced off the stage, trailing clouds of soap-bubbles behind her.

'Well, I never!' I said admiringly. 'I'll bet neither of you two would have thought of that.'

'Come, Belinda,' Maggie said. 'This is no place for us.'

They rose and left. As Belinda passed she gave a twitch of her eyebrows which looked suspiciously like a wink, smiled sweetly, said, 'I rather like you like that,' and left me pondering suspiciously as to the meaning of her remark. I followed their progess to the exit to see if anyone followed them, and followed they were, first of all by a very fat, very heavily built character with enormous jowls and an air of benevolence, but this was hardly of any significance as he was immediately followed by several dozen others. The highlight of the evening was over, great moments like those came but seldom and the summits were to be rarely scaled again—except three times a night, seven nights a week—and they were off to greener pastures where hooch could be purchased at a quarter of the price.

The club was half-empty now, the pall of smoke thinning and the visibility correspondingly improving. I looked around but in this momentary lull in the proceedings saw nothing of interest. Waiters circulated. I ordered a Scotch and was given a drink that rigorous chemical analysis might have found to contain a trace element of whisky. An old man mopped the tiny dance floor with the deliberate and stylized movements of a priest performing sacred rites. The band, mercifully silent, enthusiastically quaffed beer presented them by some tone-deaf customer. And then I saw the person I'd come to see, only it looked as if I wouldn't be seeing her for very long.

Astrid Lemay was standing in an inner doorway at the back end of a room, pulling a wrap around her shoulders while another girl whispered in her ear; from their tense expressions and hurried movements it appeared to be a message of some urgency. Astrid nodded several times, then almost ran across the tiny dance floor and passed through the front entrance. Somewhat more leisurely, I followed her.

I closed up on her and was only a few feet behind as she turned into the Rembrandtplein. She stopped. I stopped, looked at what she was looking at and listened to what she was listening to.

The barrel-organ was parked in the street outside a roofed-in, overhead-heated but windowless sidewalk café. Even at that time of night the café was almost full and the suffering customers had about them the look of people about to pay someone large sums of money to move elsewhere. This organ appeared to be a replica of the one outside the Rembrandt, with the same garish colour scheme, multi-coloured canopy and identically dressed puppets dancing at the end of their elasticized strings, although this machine was clearly inferior, mechanically and musically, to the Rembrandt one. This machine, too, was manned by an ancient, but this one sported a foot-long flowing grey beard that had neither been washed nor combed since he'd stopped shaving and who wore a stetson hat and a British Army great-coat which fitted snugly around his ankles. Amidst the clankings, groanings and wheezings emitted by the organ I thought I detected an excerpt from *La Bohème*, although heaven knew that Puccini never made the dying Mimi suffer the way she would have suffered had she been in the Rembrandtplein that night.

The ancient had a close and apparently attentive audience of one. I recognized him as being one of the group I had seen by the organ outside the Rembrandt. His clothes were threadbare but neatly kept, his lanky black hair tumbled down to his painfully thin shoulders, the blades of which protruded through his jacket like sticks. Even at that distance of about twenty feet I could see that his degree of emaciation was advanced. I could see only part of one side of the face, but that little showed a cadaverously sunken cheek with skin the colour of old parchment.

He was leaning on the end of the barrel-organ, but not from any love of Mimi. He was leaning on the barrel-organ because if he hadn't leaned on something he would surely have fallen down. He was obviously a very sick young man indeed with total collapse only one unpremeditated move away. Occasionally his whole body was convulsed by uncontrollable spasms of shaking: less frequently he made harsh sobbing or guttural noises in his throat. Clearly the old man in the great-coat did not regard him as being very good for business for he kept hovering around him indecisively, making reproachful clucking noises and ineffectual movements of his arms, very much like a rather demented hen. He also kept glancing over his shoulder and apprehensively round the square as if he were afraid of something or someone.

Astrid walked quickly towards the barrel-organ with myself close behind. She smiled apologetically at the bearded ancient, put her arm around the young man and pulled him away from the organ. Momentarily he tried to straighten up and I could see that he was a pretty tall

94

youngster, at least six inches taller than the girl: his height served only to accentuate his skeleton frame. His eyes were staring and glazed and his face the face of a man dying from starvation, his cheeks so incredibly hollowed that one would have sworn that he could have no teeth. Astrid tried to half lead, half carry him away, but though his emaciation had reached a degree where he could scarcely be any heavier than the girl, if at all, his uncontrollable lurching made her stagger across the pavement.

I approached them without a word, put my arm round him—it was like putting my arm round a skeleton—and took his weight off Astrid. She looked at me and the brown eyes were sick with anxiety and fear. I don't suppose my sepia complexion gave her much confidence either.

'Please!' Her voice was beseeching. 'Please leave me. I can manage.'

'You can't. He's a very sick boy, Miss Lemay.'

She stared at me. 'Mr Sherman!'

'I'm not sure if I like that,' I said reflectively. 'An hour or two ago you'd never seen me, never even knew my name. But now that I've gone all sun-tanned and attractive—Oops!'

George, whose rubbery legs had suddenly turned to jelly, had almost slipped from my grip. I could see that the two of us weren't going to get very far waltzing like this along the Rembrandtplein, so I stooped down to hoist him over my shoulder in a fireman's lift. She caught my arm in panic.

'No! Don't do that! Don't do that!'

'Why ever not?' I said reasonably. 'It's easier this way.'

'No, no! If the police see you they will take him away.'

I straightened, put my arm around him again and tried to maintain him as near to the vertical as was possible. 'The hunter and the hunted,' I said. 'You and van Gelder both.'

'Please?'

'And of course, brother George is—'

'How do you know his name?' she whispered.

'It's my business to know things,' I said loftily. 'As I was saying, brother George is under the further disadvantage of not being exactly unknown to the police. Having an ex-convict for a brother can be a distinct disadvantage.'

She made no reply. I doubt if I've ever seen anyone who looked so completely miserable and defeated.

'Where does he live?' I asked.

'With me, of course.' The question seemed to surprise her. 'It's not far.'

It wasn't either, not more than fifty yards down a side-street—if so narrow and gloomy a lane could be called a street—past the Balinova. The stairs up to Astrid's flat were the narrowest and most twisted I had ever come across, and with George slung over my shoulder I had difficulty in negotiating them. Astrid unlocked the door to her flat, which proved to be hardly larger than a rabbit-hutch, consisting, as far as I could see, of a tiny sitting-room with an equally tiny bedroom leading off it. I went through to the bedroom, laid George on the narrow bed, straightened and mopped my brow.

'I've climbed better ladders than those damned stairs of yours,' I said feelingly.

'I'm sorry. The girls' hostel is cheaper, but with George . . . They don't pay very highly at the Balinova.'

It was obvious from the two tiny rooms, neat but thread-bare like George's clothes, that they paid very little. I said: 'People in your position are lucky to get anything.'

'Please?'

'Not so much of the "please" stuff. You know damned well what I mean. Don't you, Miss Lemay—or may I call you Astrid?'

'How do you know my name?' Off-hand I couldn't ever recall having seen a girl wring her hands but that's what she was doing now. 'How—how do you know things about me?'

'Come off it,' I said roughly. 'Give some credit to your boy-friend.'

'Boy-friend? I haven't got a boy-friend.'

'Ex-boy-friend, then. Or does "late boy-friend" suit you better?'

'Jimmy?' she whispered.

'Jimmy Duclos,' I nodded. 'He may have fallen for you —fatally fallen for you—but he'd already told me something about you. I even have a picture of you.'

She seemed confused. 'But—but at the airport—'

'What *did* you expect me to do—embrace you? Jimmy was killed at the airport because he was on to something. What was that something?'

'I'm sorry. I can't help you.'

'Can't? Or won't?'

She made no reply.

'Did you love him, Astrid? Jimmy?'

She looked at me dumbly, her eyes glistening. She nodded slowly.

'And you won't tell me?' Silence. I sighed and tried another tack. 'Did Jimmy Duclos tell you what he was?'

She shook her head.

'But you guessed?'

She nodded.

'And told someone what you guessed.'

This got her. 'No! No! I told nobody. Before God, I told nobody!' She'd loved him, all right, and she wasn't lying.

'Did he ever mention me?'

'No.'

'But you know who I am?'

She just looked at me, two big tears trickling slowly down her cheeks.

'You know damn well that I run Interpol's narcotics bureau in London.'

More silence. I caught her shoulders and shook her angrily. 'Well, don't you?'

She nodded. A great girl for silences.

'Then if Jimmy didn't tell you, who did?'

'Oh God! Please leave me alone!' A whole lot of other tears were chasing the first two down her cheeks now. It was her day for crying and mine for sighing, so I sighed and changed my tack again and looked through the door at the boy on the bed.

'I take it,' I said, 'that George is not the breadwinner of the family?'

'George cannot work.' She said it as if she were stating a simple law of nature. 'He hasn't worked for over a year. But what has George to do with this?'

'George has everything to do with it.' I went and bent over him, looked at him closely, lifted an eyelid and dropped it again. 'What do you do for him when he's like this?'

'There is nothing one can do.'

I pushed the sleeve up George's skeleton-like arm. Punctured, mottled and discoloured from innumerable injections, it was a revolting sight: Trudi's had been nothing compared to this. I said: 'There's nothing anyone will ever be able to do for him. You know that, don't you?'

'I know that.' She caught my speculative look, stopped dabbing her face with a lace handkerchief about the size of a postage stamp and smiled bitterly. 'You want me to roll up *my* sleeve.'

'I don't insult nice girls. What I want to do is to ask you some simple questions that you can answer. How long has George been like this?'

'Three years.'

'How long have you been in the Balinova?'

'Three years.'

'Like it there?'

'Like it?' This girl gave herself away every time she opened her mouth. 'Do you know what it *is* to work in a night-club—a night-club like that? Horrible, nasty, lonely old men leering at you—'

'Jimmy Duclos wasn't horrible or nasty or old.'

She was taken aback. 'No. No, of course not. Jimmy—'

'Jimmy Duclos is dead, Astrid. Jimmy is dead because he fell for a night-club hostess who's being blackmailed.'

'Nobody's blackmailing me.'

'No? Then who's putting the pressure on you to keep

silent, to work at a job you obviously loathe? And why are they putting pressure on you? Is it because of George here? What has he done or what do they say he has done? I know he's been in prison, so it can't be that. What is it, Astrid, that made you spy on me? Whaι do you know of Jimmy Duclos's death? I know *how* he died. But who killed him and why?'

'I didn't know he'd be killed!' She sat down on the bed-sofa, her hands covering her face, her shoulders heaving. 'I didn't *know* he would be killed.'

'All right, Astrid.' I gave up because I was achieving nothing except a mounting dislike for myself. She'd probably loved Duclos, he was only a day dead and here was I lacerating bleeding wounds. 'I've known too many people walk in the fear of death to even try to make you talk. But think about it, Astrid, for God's sake and your own sake, think about it. It's your life, and that's all that's left for you to worry about now. George has no life left.'

'There's nothing I can do, nothing I can say.' Her face was still in her hands. 'Please go.'

I didn't think there was anything more I could do or say either, so I did as she asked and left.

Clad only in trousers and singlet I looked at myself in the tiny mirror in the tiny bathroom. All traces of the stain seemed to have been removed from my face, neck and hands, which was more than I could say for the large and once-white towel I held in my hands. It was sodden and stained beyond recovery to a deep chocolate colour.

I went through the door into the bedroom that was hardly big enough to take the bed and the bed-settee it contained. The bed was occupied by Maggie and Belinda, both sitting upright, both looking very fetching in very attractive nightdresses which appeared to consist mainly of holes. But I'd more urgent problems on my mind at the moment than the way in which some night-wear manufacturers skimped on their material.

'You've ruined our towel,' Belinda complained.

'Tell them you were removing your make-up.' I reached

for my shirt, which was a deep russet colour all round the
inside of the neck-band, but there was nothing I could do
about that. 'So most of the night-club girls live in this
Hostel Paris?'

Maggie nodded. 'So Mary said.'

'So Mary said.'

'Mary?'

'This nice English girl working in the Trianon.'

'There are no nice English girls working in the Trianon,
only naughty English girls. Was she one of the girls in
church?' Maggie shook her head. 'Well, that at least bears
out what Astrid said.'

'Astrid?' Belinda said. 'You spoke to her?'

'I passed the time of day with her. Not very profitably,
I'm afraid. She wasn't communicative.' I told them briefly
how uncommunicative she'd been, then went on: 'Well, it's
time you two started doing a little work instead of hanging
about night-clubs.' They looked at each other, then coldly at
me. 'Maggie, take a stroll in the Vondel Park tomorrow. See
if Trudi is there—you know her. Don't let her see you
—she knows you. See what she does, if she meets
anyone, talks to anyone: it's a big park but you should
have little difficulty in locating her if she's there—she'll be
accompanied by an old dear who's about five feet round the
middle. Belinda, keep tabs on that hostel tomorrow evening. If you recognize any girl who was in the church, follow
her and see what she's up to.' I shrugged into my very
damp jacket. 'Good night.'

'That was all? You're off?' Maggie seemed faintly surprised.

'My, you are in a hurry,' Belinda said.

'Tomorrow night,' I promised, 'I'll tuck you both in and
tell you all about Goldilocks and the three bears. Tonight I
have things to attend to.'

CHAPTER SEVEN

I parked the police car on top of a 'No parking' sign painted on the road and walked the last hundred yards to the hotel. The barrel-organ had gone to wherever barrel-organs go in the watches of the night, and the foyer was deserted except for the assistant manager who was sitting dozing in a chair behind the desk. I reached over, quietly unhooked the key and walked up the first two flights of stairs before taking the lift in case I waked the assistant manager from what appeared to be a sound—and no doubt well-deserved —sleep.

I took off my wet clothes—which meant all of them— showered, put on a dry outfit, went down by lift and banged my room key noisily on the desk. The assistant manager blinked himself awake, looked at me, his watch and the key in that order.

'Mr Sherman. I—I didn't hear you come in.'

'Hours ago. You were asleep. This quality of childlike innocence—'

He wasn't listening to me. For a second time he peered fuzzily at his watch.

'What are you doing, Mr Sherman?'

'I am sleep-walking.'

'It's half-past two in the morning!'

'I don't sleep-walk during the day,' I said reasonably. I turned and peered through the vestibule. 'What? No door- man, no porter, no taximan, no organ-grinder, not a tail or shadow in sight. Lax. Remiss. You will be held to account for this negligence.'

'Please?'

'Eternal vigilance is the price of admiralty.'

'I do not understand.'

'I'm not sure I do either. Are there any barbers open at this time of night?'

'Are there any—did you say—'

101

'Never mind. I'm sure I'll find one somewhere.'

I left. Twenty yards from the hotel I stepped into a door-way, cheerfully prepared to clobber anyone who seemed bent on following me, but after two or three minutes it became clear that no one was. I retrieved my car and drove down towards the docks area, parking it some distance and two streets away from the First Reformed Church of the American Huguenot Society. I walked down to the canal.

The canal, lined with the inevitable elm and lime trees, was dark and brown and still and reflected no light at all from the dimly-lit narrow streets on either side. Not one building on either side of the canal showed a light. The church looked more dilapidated and unsafe than ever and had about it that strange quality of stillness and remoteness and watchfulness that many churches seem to possess at night. The huge crane with its massive boom was silhouetted menacingly against the night sky. The absence of any indication of life was total. All that was lacking was a cemetery.

I crossed the street, mounted the steps and tried the church door. It was unlocked. There was no reason why it should have been locked but I found it vaguely surprising that it wasn't. The hinges must have been well-oiled for the door opened and closed soundlessly.

I switched on the torch and made a quick 360° traverse. I was alone. I made a more methodical inspection. The interior was small, even smaller than one would have guessed from outside, blackened and ancient, so ancient that I could see that the oaken pews had originally been fashioned by adzes. I lifted the beam of the torch but there was no balcony, just half-a-dozen small dusty stained-glass windows that even on a sunny day could have ad-mitted only a minimal quantity of light. The entrance door was the only external door to the church. The only other door was in a corner at the top end of the church, half-way between the pulpit and an antique bellows-operated organ.

I made for this door, laid my hand on the knob and switched off the torch. This door creaked, but not loudly. I stepped forward cautiously and softly and it was as well that I did for what I stepped on was not another floor beyond but the first step in a flight of descending stairs. I followed those steps down, eighteen of them in a complete circle and moved forward gingerly, my hand extended in front of me to locate the door which I felt must be in front of me. But there was no door in front of me. I switched on my torch.

The room I found myself in was about half the size of the church above. I made another quick circuit with the torch. There were no windows here, just two naked overhead lights. I located the switch and switched it on. The room was even more blackened than the church proper. The rough wooden floor was filthy with the trampled dirt of countless years. There were some tables and chairs in the centre of the room and the two side walls were lined with half-booths, very narrow and very high. The place looked like a medieval café.

I felt my nostrils twitch involuntarily at a well-remembered and unloved smell. It could have come from anywhere but I fancied it came from the row of booths on my right. I put my torch away, took my pistol from its felt underarm holster, dug in a pocket for a silencer and screwed it on. I walked cat-footed across the room and my nose told me that I was heading in the right direction. The first booth was empty. So was the second. Then I heard the sound of breathing. I moved forward with millimetric stealth and my left eye and the barrel of the pistol went round the corner of the third booth at the same instant.

My precautions were unnecessary. No danger offered here. Two things rested on the narrow deal table, an ashtray with a cigarette end burnt away to the butt, and the arms and head of a man who was slumped forward, sound asleep, his face turned away from me. I didn't have to see- his face. George's gaunt frame and threadbare clothes were unmistakable. Last time I'd seen him I'd have sworn that he would have been unable to stir from his bed for the next twenty-four hours—or I would have sworn, had he been a normal person. But junkies in an advanced state of addiction are as far from normal as any person can ever become and are capable of astonishing if very brief feats of recovery. I left him where he was. For the moment, he presented no problem.

There was a door at the end of this room between the two rows of booths. I opened it, with rather less care than previously, went inside, located a switch and pressed it.

This was a wide but very narrow room, running the full width of the church but no more than ten feet across. Both sides of the room were lined with shelves and those shelves were stacked high with Bibles. It came as no surprise to discover that they were replicas of those I had examined in the warehouse of Morgenstern and Muggenthaler, the ones that the First Reformed Church handed out with such liberality to the Amsterdam hotels. There didn't seem to be anything to be gained by having another look at them so I stuck my gun in my belt and went ahead and looked at them anyway. I picked several at random from the front row on a shelf and flicked through them: they were as innocuous as Bibles can be, which is as innocuous as you can get. I jerked into the second row and the same cursory examination yielded up the same result. I pushed part of the second row to one side and picked up a Bible from the third row.

This copy may or may not have been innocuous, depending upon your interpretation of the reason for its savagely multilated state, but as a Bible as such it was a complete failure because the hole that had been smoothly scooped out from its centre extended almost the entire width of the book: the hole itself was about the size and shape of a large fig. I examined several more Bibles from the same row: all had the same hollowed out centre, obviously machine-made. Keeping one of the mutilated copies to one side, I replaced the other Bibles as I had found them and moved towards the door opposite the one by which I'd entered the narrow room. I opened it and pressed the light switch.

The First Reformed Church, I had to admit, had certainly done their level and eminently successful best to comply with the exhortations of the avant-garde clergy of today that it was the Church's duty to keep abreast with and participate in the technological age in which we live. Conceivably, they might have expected to be taken a degree less literally, but then unspecified exhortation, when translated into practice, is always liable to a certain amount of executive misdirection, which appeared to be what had happened in this case: this room, which took up nearly half the basement area of the church, was, in fact, a superbly equipped machine shop.

To my untrained eye, it had everything—lathes, milling machines, presses, crucibles, moulds, a furnace, a large stamping machine and benches to which were bolted a number of smaller machines whose purpose was a mystery to me. One end of the floor was covered with what appeared to be brass and copper shavings, for the main part lying in tightly twisted coils. In a bin in one corner lay a large and untidy heap of lead pipes, all evidently old, and some rolls of used lead roof sheathing. Altogether, a highly functional place and one clearly devoted to manufacture: what the end products were was anyone's guess for certainly no examples of them were lying around.

I was half-way along the room, walking slowly, when I as much imagined as heard the very faintest sensation of sound from about the area of the doorway I'd just passed through: and I could feel again that uncomfortable tingling sensation in the back of my neck: someone was examining it, and with no friendly intent, from a distance of only a very few yards.

I walked on unconcernedly, which is no easy thing to do when the chances are good that the next step you take may be anticipated by a .38 bullet or something equally lethal in the base of the skull, but walk I did, for to turn round armed with nothing but a hollowed-out Bible in my left hand—my gun was still in my belt—seemed a sure way of precipitating that involuntary pressure of the nervous trigger-finger. I had behaved like a moron, with a blundering idiocy for which I would have bawled out anyone else, and it looked very much as if I might pay the moron's price. The unlocked main door, the unlocked door leading

105

to the basement, the access free and open to anyone who might care to investigate bespoke only one thing: the presence of a quiet man with a gun whose job it was not to prevent entry but to prevent departure in the most permanent way. I wondered where he had been hiding, perhaps in the pulpit, perhaps in some side door leading off the stairs, the existence or otherwise of which I'd been too careless to investigate.

I reached the end of the room, glanced slightly to my left behind the end lathe, made a slight murmur of surprise and stooped low behind the lathe. I didn't stay in that position for more than two seconds for there seemed little point in postponing what I knew must be inevitable: when I lifted the top of my head quickly above the lathe, the barrel of my silenced gun was already lined up with my right eye.

He was no more than fifteen feet away, advancing on soundless rubber moccasins, a wizened, rodent-faced figure of a man, with a paper-white face and glowing dark-coal eyes. What he was pointing in the general direction of the lathe in front of me was far worse than any .38 pistol, it was a blood-chilling whippet, a double-barrelled twelve-bore shotgun sawn off at both barrels and stock, probably the most lethally effective short-range weapon ever devised.

I saw him and squeezed the trigger of my gun in the same moment, for if anything was certain it was that I would never be given a second moment.

A red rose bloomed in the centre of the wizened man's forehead. He took one step back, the reflex step of a man already dead, and crumpled to the floor almost as soundlessly as he had been advancing towards me, the whippet still clutched in his hand. I switched my eyes towards the door but if there were any reinforcements to hand they were prudently concealing the fact. I straightened and went quickly across the room to where the Bibles were stored, but there was no one there nor was there in any of the booths in the next room where George was still lying unconscious across his table.

I hauled George none too gently from his seat, got him

over my shoulder, carried him upstairs to the church proper
and dumped him unceremoniously behind the pulpit where
he would be out of sight of anyone who might glance in
casually from the main door, although why anyone should
take it into his head to glance in at that time of night I
couldn't imagine. I opened the main door and glanced
out, although far from casually, but the canal street was
deserted in both directions.

Three minutes later I had the taxi parked not far from
the church. I went inside, retrieved George, dragged him
down the steps and across the road and bundled him into
the back seat of the taxi. He promptly fell off the seat on
to the floor and as he was probably safer in that position I
left him there, quickly checked that no one was taking any
interest in what I was doing and went back inside the
church again.

The dead man's pockets yielded nothing except a few
homemade cigarettes which accorded well enough with the
fact that he had obviously been hopped to the eyes when he
had come after me with the whippet. I took the whippet in
my left hand, seized the dead man by the collar of his
coat—any other method of conveying him from there
would have resulted in a blood-stained suit and this was the
only serviceable suit I'd left—and dragged him across
the basement and up the stairs, closing doors and putting
out lights as I went.

Again the cautious reconnaissance at the church main
door, again the deserted street. I dragged the man across
the street into what little cover was offered by the taxi and
lowered him into the canal as soundlessly as he would
doubtless have lowered me if he'd been a bit handier with
the whippet, which I now lowered into the canal after him.
I went back to the taxi and was about to open the driver's
door when a door of the house next to the church swung
wide and a man appeared, who looked around uncertainly
and then made his way across to where I was standing.

He was a big, burly character dressed in what appeared
to be some kind of voluminous night-gown with a bathing
wrap over it. He had rather an impressive head, with a

splendid mane of white hair, a white moustache, a pink-cheeked healthy complexion and, at that moment, an air of slightly bemused benevolence.

'Can I be of help?' He had the deep resonant modulated voice of one obviously accustomed to hearing quite a lot of it. 'Is there something wrong?'

'What should be wrong?'

'I thought I heard a noise coming from the church.'

'The church?' It was my turn to look bemused.

'Yes. My church. There.' He pointed to it in case I couldn't recognize a church when I saw one. 'I'm the pastor. Goodbody. Dr Thaddeus Goodbody. I thought some intruder was perhaps moving around—'

'Not me, Reverend. I haven't been inside a church for years.'

He nodded as if he weren't at all surprised. 'We live in a godless age. A strange hour to be abroad, young man.'

'Not for a taxi-driver on the night shift.'

He looked at me with an unconvinced expression and peered into the back of the taxi. 'Merciful heavens. There's a body on the floor.'

'There isn't a body on the floor. There's a drunken sailor on the floor and I'm taking him back to his ship. He just fell to the floor a few seconds ago so I stopped to get him back on his seat again. I thought,' I added virtuously, 'that it would be the Christian thing to do. With a corpse, I wouldn't bother.'

My professional appeal availed nothing. He said, in the tone which he presumably kept for reproaching the more backsliding of his flock : 'I insist on seeing for myself.'

He pressed firmly forward and I pressed him firmly back again. I said : 'Don't make me lose my licence. Please.'

'I knew it! I knew it! Something is far amiss. So I can make you lose your licence?'

'Yes. If I throw you into the canal then I'll lose my licence. If, that is,' I added consideringly, 'you manage to climb back out again.'

'What! The canal! Me? A man of God? Are you threatening me with violence, sir?'

'Yes.'

Dr Goodbody backed off several rapid paces.

'I have your licence, sir. I shall report you—'

The night was wearing on and I wanted some sleep before the morning, so I climbed into the car and drove off. He was shaking his fist at me in a fashion that didn't say much for his concept of brotherly love and appeared to be delivering himself of some vehement harangue but I couldn't hear any of it. I wondered if he would lodge a complaint with the police and thought that the odds were against it.

I was getting tired of carrying George up stairs. True, he weighed hardly anything at all, but what with the lack of sleep and dinner I was a good way below par and, moreover, I'd had my bellyful of junkies. I found the door to Astrid's tiny flat unlocked, which was what I would have expected to find if George had been the last person to use it. I opened it, switched on the light, walked past the sleeping girl, and deposited George none too gently on his own bed. I think it must have been the noise the mattress made and not the bright overhead light in her room that wakened Astrid: in any event, she was sitting up in her bed-settee and rubbing eyes still bemused from sleep as I returned to her room. I looked down at her in what I hoped was a speculative fashion and said nothing.

'He was asleep, then I went to sleep,' she said defensively. 'He must have got up and gone out again.' When I treated this masterpiece of deduction with the silence it deserved she went on almost desperately: 'I didn't hear him go out. I didn't. Where did you find him?'

'You'd never guess, I'm sure. In a garage, over a barrel-organ, trying to get the cover off. He wasn't making much progress.'

As she had done earlier that night, she buried her face in her hands: this time she wasn't crying, although I supposed drearily that it would be only a matter of time.

'What's so upsetting about that?' I asked. 'He's very interested in barrel-organs, isn't he, Astrid? I wonder why. It is curious. He's musical, perhaps?'

'No. Yes. Ever since he was a little boy—'

'Oh, be quiet. If he was musical he'd rather listen to a pneumatic drill. There's a very simple reason why he dotes on those organs. Very simple—and both you and I know what it is.'

She stared at me, not in surprise: her eyes were sick with fear. Wearily, I sank down on the edge of the bed and took both her hands in mine.

'Astrid?'

'Yes?'

'You're almost as accomplished a liar as I am. You didn't go looking for George because you knew damn well where George was and you know damn well where I found him, in a place where he was safe and sound, in a place where the police would never find him because they would never think to look for anyone there.' I sighed. 'A smoke is not the needle, but I suppose it's better than nothing.'

She looked at me with a stricken face, then got back to burying her face in her hands. Her shoulders shook as I knew they would. How obscure or what my motives were I didn't know, I just couldn't sit there without holding out at least a tentatively comforting hand and when I did she looked up at me numbly through tear-filled eyes, reached up her hands and sobbed bitterly on my shoulder. I was becoming accustomed to this treatment in Amsterdam but still far from reconciled to it, so I tried to ease her arms gently away but she only tightened them the more. It had, I knew, nothing whatsoever to do with me: for the moment she needed something to cling to and I happened to be there. Gradually the sobs eased and she lay there, her tear-stained face defenceless and full of despair.

I said: 'It's not too late, Astrid.'

'That's not true. You know as well as I know, it was too late from the beginning.'

'For George, yes, it is. But don't you see I'm trying to help you?'

'How can you help me?'

'By destroying the people who have destroyed your
110

brother. By destroying the people who are destroying
you. But I need help. In the end, we all need help—you,
me, everyone. Help me—and I'll help you. I promise
you, Astrid.'

I wouldn't say that the despair in her face was replaced
by some other expression but at least it seemed to become
a degree less total as she nodded once or twice, smiled
shakily and said: 'You seem very good at destroying
people.'

'You may have to be, too,' I said and I gave her a very
small gun, a Lilliput, the effectiveness of which belies its
tiny .21 bore.

I left ten minutes later. As I came out into the street I saw
two shabbily dressed men sitting on a step in a doorway
almost opposite, arguing heatedly but not loudly so I
transferred my gun to my pocket and walked across to
where they were. Ten feet away I sheered off for the
pungent odour of rum in the air was so overwhelming as
to give rise to the thought that they hadn't so much been
drinking the stuff but were newly arisen from immersion
in a vat of the best Demerara. I was beginning to see
spooks in every flickering shadow and what I needed was
sleep, so I collected the taxi, drove back to the hotel and
went to sleep.

CHAPTER EIGHT

Remarkably, the sun was shining when my portable alarm went off the following morning—or the same morning. I showered, shaved, dressed, went downstairs and breakfasted in the restaurant with such restoring effect that I was able to smile at and say a civil good morning to the assistant manager, the doorman and the barrel-organ attendant in that order. I stood for a minute or two outside the hotel looking keenly around me with the air of a man waiting for his shadow to turn up, but it seemed that discouragement had set in and I was able to make my unaccompanied way to where I'd left the police taxi the previous night. Even though, in broad daylight, I'd stopped staring at shadows I opened the hood all the same but no one had fixed any lethal explosive device during the night so I drove off and arrived at the Marnixstraat HQ at precisely ten o'clock, the promised time.

Colonel de Graaf, complete with search warrant, was waiting for me in the street. So was Inspector van Gelder. Both men greeted me with the courteous restraint of those who think their time is being wasted but are too polite to say so and led me to a chauffeur-driven police car which was a great deal more luxurious than the one they'd given me.

'You still think our visit to Morgenstern and Muggenthaler is desirable?' de Graaf asked. 'And necessary?'

'More so than ever.'

'Something has happened? To make you feel that way?'

'No,' I lied. I touched my head. 'I'm fey at times.'

De Graaf and van Gelder looked briefly at each other. 'Fey?' de Graaf said carefully.

'I get premonitions.'

There was another brief interchange of glances to indicate their mutal opinion of police officers who operated on this scientific basis, then de Graaf said, circumspectly

112

changing the topic: 'We have eight plain-clothes officers standing by down there in a plain van. But you say you don't really want the place searched?'

'I want it searched all right—rather, I want to give the appearance of a search. What I really want are the invoices giving a list of all the suppliers of souvenir items to the warehouse.'

'I hope you know what you are doing,' van Gelder said. He sounded grave.

'*You* hope,' I said. 'How do you think *I* feel?'

Neither of them said how they thought I felt, and as it seemed that the line of conversation was taking an unprofitable turn we all kept quiet until we arrived at our destination. We drew up outside the warehouse behind a nondescript grey van and got out and as we did a man in a dark suit climbed down from the front of the grey van and approached us. His civilian suit didn't do much for him as disguise went: I could have picked him out as a cop at fifty yards.

He said to de Graaf: 'We're ready, sir.'

'Bring your men.'

'Yes, sir.' The policeman pointed upwards. 'What do you make of that sir?'

We followed the direction of his arm. There was a wind blowing gustily that morning, nothing much but enough to give a slow if rather erratic pendulum swing to a gaily coloured object suspended from the hoisting beam at the top of the warehouse: it swung through an arc of about four feet and was, in its setting, one of the most gruesome things I had ever encountered.

Unmistakably, it was a puppet, and a very large puppet at that, well over three feet tall and dressed, inevitably, in the usual immaculate and beautifully tailored traditional Dutch costume, the long striped skirt billowing coquettishly in the wind. Normally, wires or ropes are used to pass through the pulleys of hoisting beams but in this instance someone had elected to use a chain instead: the puppet was secured to the chain by what could be seen, even at that elevation, to be a wicked-looking hook, a hook that

113

was fractionally too small for the neck it passed round, so small that it had obviously had to be forced into position for the neck had been crushed at one side so that the head leaned over at a grotesque angle, almost touching the right shoulder. It was, after all, no more than a mutilated doll: but the effect was horrifying to the point of obscenity. And obviously I wasn't the only one who felt that way.

'What a macabre sight.' De Graaf sounded shocked and he looked it too. 'What in the name of God is that for? What—what's the point of it, what's the purpose behind it? What kind of sick mind could perpetrate an —an obscenity like that?'

Van Gelder shook his head. 'Sick minds are everywhere and Amsterdam has its fair share. A jilted sweetheart, a hated mother-in-law—'

'Yes, yes, those are legion. But this—this is abnormality to the point of insanity. To express your feelings in this terrible way.' He looked at me oddly, as if he were having second thoughts about the purposelessness of this visit. 'Major Sherman, doesn't it strike you as very strange—'

'It strikes me the way it strikes you. The character responsible has a cast-iron claim to the first vacancy in a psychotic ward. But that isn't why I came here.'

'Of course not, of course not.' De Graaf had a last long look at the dangling puppet, as if he could hardly force himself to look away, then gestured abruptly with his head and led the way up the steps towards the warehouse. A porter of sorts took us to the second floor and then to the office in the corner which, unlike the last time I had seen it, now had its time-locked door hospitably open.

The office, in sharp contrast to the warehouse itself, was spacious and uncluttered and modern and comfortable, beautifully carpeted and draped in different shades of lime and equipped with very expensive up-to-the-minute Scandinavian furniture more appropriate to a luxurious lounge than to a dock-side office. Two men seated in deep armchairs behind separate large and leather-covered desks rose courteously to their feet and ushered de Graaf,

114

van Gelder and myself into other and equally restful armchairs while they themselves remained standing. I was glad they did, for this way I could have a better look at them and they were both, in their way, very similar, well worth looking at. But I didn't wait more than a few seconds to luxuriate in the warmth of their beaming reception.

I said to de Graaf: 'I have forgotten something very important. It is imperative I make a call on a friend immediately.' It was, too: I don't often get this chilled and leaden feeling in the stomach but when I do I'm anxious to take remedial action with the least delay.

De Graaf looked his surprise. 'A matter so important, it could have slipped your mind?'

'I have other things on my mind. This just came into it.' Which was the truth.

'A phone call, perhaps—'

'No, no. Must be personal.'

'You couldn't tell me the nature—'

'Colonel de Graaf!' He nodded in quick understanding, appreciating the fact that I wouldn't be likely to divulge State secrets in the presence of the proprietors of a warehouse about which I obviously held serious reservations. 'I could borrow your car and driver—'

'Certainly,' he said unenthusiastically.

'And if you could wait till I come back before—'

'You ask a great deal, Mr Sherman.'

'I know. But I'll only be minutes.'

I was only minutes. I had the driver stop at the first café we came to, went inside and used their public telephone. I heard the dialling tone and could feel my shoulders sag with relief as the receiver at the other end, after relay through an hotel desk, was picked up almost immediately. I said: 'Maggie?'

'Good morning, Major Sherman.' Always polite and punctilious was Maggie and I was never more glad to hear her so.

'I'm glad I caught you. I was afraid that you and Belinda might already have left—she hasn't left, has she?' I was much more afraid of several other things but this wasn't the time to tell her.

'She's still here,' Maggie said placidly.

'I want you both to leave your hotel at once. When I say at once, I mean within ten minutes. Five, if possible.'

'Leave? You mean—'

'I mean pack up, check out and don't ever go near it again. Go to another hotel. Any hotel . . . No, you blithering idiot, not mine. A suitable hotel. Take as many taxis as you like, make sure you're not followed. Telephone the number to the office of Colonel de Graaf in the Marnixstraat. Reverse the number.'

'Reverse it?' Maggie sounded shocked. 'You mean you don't trust the police either?'

'I don't know what you mean by "either" but I don't trust anyone, period. Once you've booked in, go look for Astrid Lemay. She'll be home—you have the address—or in the Balinova. Tell her she's to come to stay at your hotel till I tell her it's safe to move.'

'But her brother—'

'George can stay where he is. He's in no danger.' I couldn't remember later whether that statement was the sixth or seventh major mistake I'd made in Amsterdam. 'She is. If she objects, tell her you're going, on my authority, to the police about George.'

'But why should we go to the police—'

'No reason. But she's not to know that. She's so terrified that at the very mention of the word "police"—'

'That's downright cruel,' Maggie interrupted severely.

'Fiddlesticks!' I shouted and banged the phone back on its rest.

One minute later I was back in the warehouse and this time I had leisure to have a longer and closer look at the two proprietors. Both of them were almost caricatures of the foreigner's conception of the typical Amsterdamer. They were both very big, very fat, rubicund and heavily jowled men who, in the first brief introduction I had had to them, had had their faces deeply creased in lines of good-will and joviality, an expression that was now conspicuously lacking

116

in both. Evidently, de Graaf had become impatient even with my very brief absence and had started the proceedings without me. I didn't reproach him and, in return, he had the tact not to enquire how things had gone with me. Both Muggenthaler and Morgenstern were still standing in almost the identical positions in which I'd left them, gazing at each other in consternation and dismay and complete lack of understanding. Muggenthaler, who was holding a paper in his hand, let it fall to his side with a gesture of total disbelief.

'A search warrant.' The overtones of pathos and heart-break and tragedy would have moved a statue to tears; had he been half his size he'd have been a natural for Hamlet. 'A search warrant for Morgenstern and Muggenthaler! For a hundred and fifty years our two families have been respected, no, honoured tradesmen in the city of Amsterdam. And now this!' He groped behind him and sank into a chair in what appeared to be some kind of stupor, the paper falling from his hand. 'A search warrant!'

'A search warrant,' Morgenstern intoned. He, too, had found it necessary to seek an armchair. 'A search warrant, Ernest. A black day for Morgenstern and Muggenthaler! My God! The shame of it! The ignominy of it! A search warrant!'

Muggenthaler waved a despairingly listless hand. 'Go on, search all you want.'

'Don't you want to know what we're searching for?' de Graaf asked politely.

'Why should I want to know?' Muggenthaler tried to raise himself to a momentary state of indignation, but he was too stricken. 'In one hundred and fifty years—'

'Now, now, gentlemen,' de Graaf said soothingly, 'don't take it so hard. I appreciate the shock you must feel and in my own view we're on a wild goose chase. But an official request has been made and we must go through the official motions. We have information that you have illicitly obtained diamonds—'

'Diamonds!' Muggenthaler stared in disbelief at his partner. 'You hear that, Jan? Diamonds?' He shook his

117

head and said to de Graaf: 'If you find some, give me a few, will you?'

De Graaf was unaffected by the morose sarcasm. 'And, much more important, diamond-cutting machinery.'

'We're crammed from floor to ceiling with diamond-cutting machinery,' Morgenstern said heavily. 'Look for yourselves.'

'And the invoice books?'

'Anything, anything,' Muggenthaler said wearily.

'Thank you for your co-operation.' De Graaf nodded to van Gelder, who rose and left the room. De Graaf went on confidentially: 'I apologize, in advance, for what is, I'm sure, a complete waste of time. Candidly, I'm more interested in that horrible thing dangling by a chain from your hoisting beam. A puppet.'

'A what?' Muggenthaler demanded.

'A puppet. A big one.'

'A puppet on a chain.' Muggenthaler looked both flabbergasted and horrified, which is not an easy thing to achieve. 'In front of *our* warehouse? Jan!'

It wouldn't quite be accurate to say that we raced up the stairs, for Morgenstern and Muggenthaler weren't built along the right lines, but we made pretty good time for all that. On the third floor we found van Gelder and his men at work and at a word from de Graaf van Gelder joined us. I hoped his men didn't wear themselves out looking, for I knew they'd never find anything. They'd never even come across the smell of cannabis which had hung so heavily on that floor the previous night, although I felt that the sickly-sweet smell of some powerful flower-based air-freshener that had taken its place could scarcely be described as an improvement. But it hardly seemed the time to mention it to anyone.

The puppet, its back to us and the dark head resting on its right shoulder, was still swaying gently in the breeze. Muggenthaler, supported by Morgenstern and obviously feeling none too happy in his precarious position, reached out gingerly, caught the chain just above the hook and hauled it in sufficiently for him, not without considerable

118

difficulty, to unhook the puppet from the chain. He held it in his arms and stared down at it for long moments, then shook his head and looked up at Morgenstern.

'Jan, he who did this wicked thing, this sick, sick joke —he leaves our employment this very day.'

'This very hour,' Morgenstern corrected. His face twisted in repugnance, not at the puppet, but at what had been done to it. 'And such a beautiful puppet!'

Morgenstern was in no way exaggerating. It was indeed a beautiful puppet and not only or indeed primarily because of the wonderfully cut and fitted bodice and gown. Despite the fact that the neck had been broken and cruelly gouged by the hook, the face itself was arrestingly beautiful, a work of great artistic skill in which the colours of the dark hair, the brown eyes and the complexion blended so subtly and in which the delicate features had been so exquisitely shaped that it was hard to believe that this was the face of a puppet and not that of a human being with an existence and distinctive personality of her own. Nor was I the only person who felt that way.

De Graaf took the puppet from Muggenthaler and gazed at it. 'Beautiful,' he murmured. 'How beautiful. And how real, how living. This lives.' He glanced at Muggenthaler. 'Would you have any idea who made this puppet?'

'I've never seen one like it before. It's not one of ours, I'm sure, but the floor foreman is the man to ask. But I know it's not ours.'

'And this exquisite colouring,' de Graaf mused. 'It's so right for the face, so inevitable. No man could have created this from his own mind. Surely, surely, he must have worked from a living model, from someone he knew. Wouldn't you say so, Inspector?'

'It couldn't have been done otherwise,' van Gelder said flatly.

'I've the feeling, almost, that I've seen this face before,' de Graaf continued. 'Any of you gentlemen ever seen a girl like this?'

We all shook our heads slowly and none more slowly than I did. The old leaden feeling was back in my stomach

119

again but this time the lead was coated with a thick layer of ice. It wasn't just that the puppet bore a frighteningly accurate resemblance to Astrid Lemay: it was so lifelike, it *was* Astrid Lemay.

Fifteen minutes later, after the thorough search carried out in the warehouse had produced its predictably total negative result, de Graaf took his farewell of Muggenthaler and Morgenstern on the steps of the warehouse, while van Gelder and I stood by. Muggenthaler was back at his beaming while Morgenstern stood by his side, smiling with patronizing satisfaction. De Graaf shook hands warmly with both in turn.

'Again, a thousand apologies.' De Graaf was being almost effusive. 'Our information was about as accurate as it usually is. All records of this visit will be struck from the books.' He smiled broadly. 'The invoices will be returned to you as soon as certain interested parties have failed to find all the different illicit diamond suppliers they expected to find there. Good morning, gentlemen.'

Van Gelder and I said our farewell in turn and I shook hands especially warmly with Morgenstern and reflected that it was just as well that he lacked the obvious ability to read thoughts and had unluckily come into this world without any inborn ability to sense when death and danger stood very close at hand: for Morgenstern it was who had been at the Balinova night-club last night and had been the first to leave after Maggie and Belinda had passed out into the street.

We made the journey back to the Marnixstraat in partial silence, by which I mean that de Graaf and van Gelder talked freely but I didn't. They appeared to be much more interested in the curious incident of the broken puppet than they were in the ostensible reason for our visit to the warehouse, which probably demonstrated quite clearly what they thought of the ostensible reason, and as I hardly liked to intrude to tell them that they had their priorities right, I kept silent,

Back in his office, de Graaf said: 'Coffee? We have a girl here who makes the best coffee in Amsterdam.'

'A pleasure to be postponed. Too much of a hurry, I'm afraid.'

'You have plans? A course of action, perhaps?'

'Neither. I want to lie on my bed and think.'

'Then why—'

'Why come up here in the first place? Two small requests. Find out, please, if any telephone message has come through for me.'

'Message?'

'From this person I had to go to see when we were down in the warehouse.' I was getting so that I could hardly tell whether I was telling the truth or lying.

De Graaf nodded, picked up a phone, talked briefly, wrote down a long screed of letters and figures and handed the paper to me. The letters were meaningless: the figures, reversed, would be the girls' new telephone number. I put the paper in my pocket.

'Thank you. I'll have to decode this.'

'And the second small request?'

'Could you lend me a pair of binoculars?'

'Binoculars?'

'I want to do some bird-watching,' I explained.

'Of course,' van Gelder said heavily. 'You will recall, Major Sherman, that we are supposed to be co-operating closely?'

'Well?'

'You are not, if I may say so, being very communicative.'

'I'll communicate with you when I've something worth communicating. Don't forget that you've been working on this for over a year. I haven't been here for two days yet. Like I say, I have to go and lie down and think.'

I didn't go and lie down and think. I drove to a telephone-box which I judged to be a circumspect distance from the police headquarters and dialled the number de Graaf had given me.

The voice at the other end of the line said: 'Hotel Touring.'

I knew it but had never been inside it: it wasn't the sort of hotel that appealed to my expense account, but it was the sort of hotel I would have chosen for the two girls.

I said: 'My name is Sherman. Paul Sherman. I believe two young ladies registered with you this morning. Could I speak to them, please?'

'I'm sorry, they are out at present.' There was no worry there; if they weren't out locating or trying to locate Astrid Lemay they would be carrying out the assignment I'd given them in the early hours of the morning. The voice at the other end anticipated my next question. 'They left a message for you, Mr Sherman. I am to say that they failed to locate your mutual friend and are now looking for some other friends. I'm afraid it's a bit vague, sir.'

I thanked him and hung up. 'Help me,' I'd said to Astrid, 'and I'll help you.' It was beginning to look as if I were helping her all right, helping her into the nearest canal or coffin. I jumped into the police taxi and made a lot of enemies in the brief journey to the rather unambitious area that bordered on the Rembrandtplein.

The door to Astrid's flat was locked but I still had my belt of illegal ironmongery around my waist. Inside, the flat was as I'd first seen it, neat and tidy and threadbare. There were no signs of violence, no signs of any hurried departure. I looked in the few drawers and closets there were and it seemed to me that they were very bare of clothes indeed. But then, as Astrid had pointed out, they were very poor indeed, so that probably meant nothing. I looked everywhere in the tiny flat where a message of some sorts could have been left, but if any had been, I couldn't find it: I didn't believe any had been. I locked the front door and drove to the Balinova night-club.

For a night-club those were still the unearthly early hours of the morning and the doors, predictably, were locked. They were strong doors and remained unaffected by the hammering and the kicking that I subjected them to, which, luckily, was more than could be said for one of the people inside whose slumber I must have so irritatingly disturbed, for a key turned and the door opened a crack.

I put my foot in the crack and widened it a little, enough to see the head and shoulders of a faded blonde who was modestly clutching a wrap high at her throat: considering that the last time I had seen her she had been clad in a thin layer of transparent soap bubbles I thought that this was overdoing it a little.

'I wish to see the manager, please.'

'We don't open till six o'clock.'

'I don't want a reservation. I don't want a job. I want to see the manager. Now.'

'He's not here.'

'So. I hope your next job is as good as this one.'

'I don't understand.' No wonder they had the lights so low last night in the Balinova, in daylight that raddled face would have emptied the place like a report that one of the customers had bubonic plague. 'What do you mean, my job?'

I lowered my voice, which you have to do when you speak with solemn gravity. 'Just that you won't have any if the manager finds that I called on a matter of the greatest urgency and you refused to let me see him.'

She looked at me uncertainly then said: 'Wait here.' She tried to close the door but I was a lot stronger than she was and after a moment she gave up and went away. She came back inside thirty seconds accompanied by a man still dressed in evening clothes.

I didn't take to him at all. Like most people, I don't like snakes and this was what this man irresistibly reminded me of. He was very tall and very thin and moved with a sinuous grace. He was effeminately elegant and dandified and had the unhealthy pallor of a creature of the night. His face was of alabaster, his features smooth, his lips non-existent: the dark hair, parted in the middle, was plastered flat against his skull. His dress suit was elegantly cut but he hadn't as good a tailor as I had: the bulge under the left armpit was quite perceptible. He held a jade cigarette-holder in a thin, white, beautifully manicured hand: his face held an expression, which was probably permanent, of quietly contemptuous amusement. Just to have him look at you

123

was a good enough excuse to hit him. He blew a thin stream of cigarette smoke into the air.

'What's all this, my dear fellow?' He looked French or Italian, but he wasn't: he was English. 'We're not open, you know.'

'You are now,' I pointed out. 'You the manager?'

'I'm the manager's representative. If you care to call back later—' he puffed some more of his obnoxious smoke into the air—'much later, then we'll see—'

'I'm a lawyer from England and on urgent business.' I handed him a card saying I was a lawyer from England. 'It is essential that I see the manager at once. A great deal of money is involved.'

If such an expression as he wore could be said to soften, then his did, though you had to have a keen eye to notice the difference. 'I promise nothing, Mr Harrison.' That was the name on the card. 'Mr Durrell may be persuaded to see you.'

He moved away like a ballet dancer on his day off and was back in moments. He nodded to me and stood to one side to let me precede him down a large and dimly lit passage, an arrangement which I didn't like but had to put up with. At the end of the passage was a door opening on a brightly lit room, and as it seemed to be intended that I should enter without knocking I did just that. I noted in passing that the door was of the type that the vaults manager—if there is such a person—of the Bank of England would have rejected as being excessive to his requirements.

The interior of the room looked more than a little like a vault itself. Two large safes, tall enough for a man to walk into, were let into one wall. Another wall was given over to a battery of lockable metal cabinets of the rental left-luggage kind commonly found in railway stations. The other two walls may well have been windowless but it was impossible to be sure: they were completely covered with crimson and violet drapes.

The man sitting behind the large mahogany desk didn't look a bit like a bank manager, at any rate a British

124

banker, who typically has a healthy outdoor appearance about him owing to his penchant for golf and the short hours he spends behind his desk. This man was sallow, about eighty pounds overweight, with greasy black hair, a greasy complexion and permanently bloodshot yellowed eyes. He wore a well-cut blue alpaca suit, a large variety of rings on both hands and a welcoming smile that didn't become him at all.

'Mr Harrison?' He didn't try to rise: probably experience had convinced him that the effort wasn't worth it. 'Pleased to meet you. My name is Durrell.'

Maybe it was, but it wasn't the name he had been born with: I thought him Armenian, but couldn't be sure. But I greeted him as civilly as if his name had been Durrell.

'You have some business to discuss with me?' he beamed. Mr Durrell was cunning and knew that lawyers didn't come all the way from England without matters of weighty import, invariably of a financial nature, to discuss.

'Well, not actually with you. With one of your employees.'

The welcoming smile went into cold storage. 'With one of my employees?'

'Yes.'

'Then why bother me?'

'Because I couldn't find her at her home address. I am told she works here.'

'She?'

'Her name is Astrid Lemay.'

'Well, now.' He was suddenly more reasonable, as if he wanted to help. 'Astrid Lemay? Working here.' He frowned thoughtfully. 'We have many girls, of course—but that name?' He shook his head.

'But friends of hers told me,' I protested.

'Some mistake. Marcel?'

The snakelike man smiled his contemptuous smile. 'No one of that name here.'

'Or ever worked here?'

Marcel shrugged, walked across to a filing cabinet, produced a folder and laid it on the desk, beckoning to me. 'All the girls who work here or have done in the past year. Look for yourself.'

I didn't bother looking. I said: 'I've been misinformed. My apologies for disturbing you.'

'I suggest you try some of the other night-clubs.' Durrell, in the standard tycoon fashion, was already busy making notes on a sheet of paper to indicate that the interview was over. 'Good day, Mr Harrison.'

Marcel had already moved to the doorway. I followed, and as I passed through, turned and smiled apologetically. 'I'm really sorry—'

'Good day.' He didn't even bother to lift his head. I did some more uncertain smiling, then courteously pulled the door to behind me. It looked a good solid soundproof door.

Marcel, standing just inside the passageway, gave me his warm smile again and, not even condescending to speak, contemptuously indicated that I should precede him down the passageway. I nodded, and as I walked past him I hit him in the middle with considerable satisfaction and a great deal of force, and although I thought that was enough I hit him again, this time on the side of the neck. I took out my gun, screwed on the silencer, took the recumbent Marcel by the collar of his jacket and dragged him towards the office door which I opened with my gun-hand.

Durrell looked up from his desk. His eyes widened as much as eyes can widen when they're almost buried in folds of fat. Then his face became very still, as faces become when the owners want to conceal their thoughts or intentions.

'Don't do it,' I said. 'Don't do any of the standard clever things. Don't reach for a button, don't press any switches on the floor, and don't, please, be so naïve as to reach for the gun which you probably have in the top right-hand drawer, you being a right-handed man.'

He didn't do any of the standard clever things.

'Push your chair back two feet.'

He pushed his chair back two feet. I dropped Marcel to

the floor, reached behind me, closed the door, turned the very fancy key in the lock, then pocketed the key. I said: 'Get up.'

Durrell got up. He stood scarcely more than five feet high. In build, he closely resembled a bullfrog. I nodded to the nearer of the two large safes.

'Open it.'

'So that's it.' He was good with his face but not so good with his voice. He wasn't able to keep that tiny trace of relief out of his voice. 'Robbery, Mr Harrison.'

'Come here,' I said. He came. 'Do you know who I am?'

'Know who you are?' A look of puzzlement. 'You just told me—'

'That my name is Harrison. Who am I?'

'I don't understand.'

He screeched with pain and fingered the already bleeding welt left by the silencer of my gun.

'Who am I?'

'Sherman.' Hate was in the eyes and the thick voice. 'Interpol.'

'Open that door.'

'Impossible. I have only half the combination. Marcel here has—'

The second screech was louder, the weal on the other cheek comparably bigger.

'Open that door.'

He twiddled with the combination and pulled the door open. The safe was about 30 inches square, of a size to hold a great deal of guilders, but then, if all the tales about the Balinova were true, tales that whispered darkly of gaming-rooms and much more interesting shows in the basement and the brisk retail of items not commonly found in ordinary retail shops, the size was probably barely adequate.

I nodded to Marcel. 'Junior, here. Shove him inside.'

'In there?' He looked horrified.

'I don't want him coming to and interrupting our discussion.'

'Discussion?'

127

'Open up.'

'He'll suffocate. Ten minutes and—'

'The next time I have to ask it will be after I put a bullet through your kneecap so that you'll never walk without a stick again. Believe me?'

He believed me. Unless you're a complete fool, and Durrell wasn't, you can always tell when a man means something. He dragged Marcel inside, which was probably the hardest work he'd done in years, because he had to do quite a bit of bending and pushing to get Marcel to fit on the tiny floor of the safe in such a way that the door could be closed. The door was closed.

I searched Durrell. He'd no offensive weapon on him. The right-hand drawer of his desk predictably yielded up a large automatic of a type unknown to me, which was not unusual as I'm not very good with guns except when aiming and firing them.

'Astrid Lemay,' I said. 'She works here.'

'She works here.'

'Where is she?'

'I don't know. Before God, I don't know.' The last was almost in a scream as I'd lifted the gun again.

'You could find out?'

'How could I find out?'

'Your ignorance and reticence do you credit,' I said. 'But they are based on fear. Fear of someone, fear of something. But you'll become all knowledgeable and forthcoming when you learn to fear something else more. Open that safe.

He opened the safe. Marcel was still unconscious.

'Get inside.

'No.' The single word came out like a hoarse scream. 'I tell you, it's airtight, hermetically sealed. Two of us in there—we'll be dead in minutes if I go in there.'

'You'll be dead in seconds if you don't.'

He went inside. He was shaking now. Whoever this was, he wasn't one of the king-pins: whoever master-minded the drug racket was a man—or men—possessed of a toughness and ruthlessness that was absolute and this man was possessed of neither.

I spent the next five minutes without profit in going through every drawer and file available to me. Everything I examined appeared to be related in one way or another to legitimate business dealing, which made sense, for Durrell would be unlikely to keep documents of a more incriminating nature where the office cleaner could get her hands on them. After five minutes I opened the safe door.

Durrell had been wrong about the amount of breathable air available inside that safe. He'd overestimated. He was semi-collapsed with his knees resting on Marcel's back, which made it fortunate for Marcel that he was still unconscious. At least, I thought he was unconscious. I didn't bother to check. I caught Durrell by the shoulder and pulled. It was like pulling a bull moose out of a swamp, but he came eventually and rolled out on to the floor. He lay there for a bit, then pushed himself groggily to his knees. I waited patiently until the laboured stertorous whooping sound dropped to a mere gasping wheeze and his complexion ran through the spectrum from a bluish-violet colour to what would have been a becomingly healthy pink had I not known that his normal complexion more resembled the colour of old newspaper. I prodded him and indicated that he should get to his feet and he managed this after a few tries.

'Astrid Lemay?' I said.

'She was here this morning.' His voice came as a hoarse whisper but audible enough all the same 'She said that very urgent family matters had come up. She had to leave the country.'

'Alone?'

'No, with her brother.'

'He was here?'

'No.'

'Where did she say she was going?'

'Athens. She belonged there.'

'She came here just to tell you this?'

'She had two months' back pay due. She needed it for the fare.'

I told him to get back inside the safe. I had a little trouble with him, but he finally decided that it offered a better chance than a bullet, so he went. I didn't want to terrify him any more. I just didn't want him to hear what I was about to say.

I got through to Schiphol on a direct line, and was finally connected with the person I wanted.

'Inspector van Gelder, Police HQ here,' I said. 'An Athens flight this morning. Probably KLM. I want to check if two people, names Astrid Lemay and George Lemay, were on board. Their descriptions are as follows —what was that?'

The voice at the other end told me that they had been aboard. There had been some difficulty, apparently, about George being allowed on the flight as his condition was such that both medical and police authorities at the airport had questioned the wisdom of it, but the girl's pleading had prevailed. I thanked my informant and hung up.

I opened the door of the safe. It hadn't been shut more than a couple of minutes this time and I didn't expect to find them in such bad shape and they weren't. Durrell's complexion was no more than puce, and Marcel had not only recovered consciousness but recovered it to the extent of trying to lug out his underarm gun, which I had carelessly forgotten to remove. As I took the gun from him before he could damage himself with it, I reflected that Marcel must have the most remarkable powers of recuperation. I was to remember this with bitter chagrin on an occasion that was to be a day or so later and very much more inauspicious for me.

I left them both sitting on the floor, and as there didn't seem to be anything worthwhile to say none of the three of us said it. I unlocked the door, opened it, closed and locked it behind me, smiled pleasantly at the faded blonde and dropped the key through a street grille outside the Balinova. Even if there wasn't a spare key available, there were telephones and alarm bells still operating from inside that room and it shouldn't take an oxyacetylene torch more than two or three hours to open it. There should be enough air inside the room to last that time. But it didn't seem very important one way or another.

I drove back to Astrid's flat and did what I should have done in the first place—asked some of her immediate neighbours if they had seen her that morning. Two had, and their stories checked. Astrid and George with two or three cases had left two hours previously in a taxi.

Astrid had skipped and I felt a bit sad and empty about it, not because she had said she would help me and hadn't but because she had closed the last escape door open to her.

Her masters hadn't killed her for two reasons. They knew I could have tied them up with her death and that would be coming too close to home. And they didn't have to because she was gone and no longer a danger to them: fear, if it is sufficiently great, can seal lips as effectively as death.

I'd liked her and would have liked to see her happy again. I couldn't blame her. For her, all the doors had been closed.

CHAPTER NINE

The view from the top of the towering Havengebouw, the skyscraper in the harbour, is unquestionably the best in Amsterdam. But I wasn't interested in the view that morning, only in the facilities this vantage point had to offer. The sun was shining, but it was breezy and cool at that altitude and even at sea-level the wind was strong enough to ruffle the blue-grey waters into irregular wavy patterns of white horses.

The observation platform was crowded with tourists, for the most part with wind-blown hair, binoculars and cameras, and although I didn't carry any camera I didn't think I looked different from any other tourist. Only my purpose in being up there was.

I leaned on my elbows and gazed out to sea. De Graaf had certainly done me proud with those binoculars, they were as good as any I had ever come across and with the near-perfect visibility that day the degree of definition was all that I could ever have wished for.

The glasses were steadied on a coastal steamer of about a thousand tons that was curving into harbour. Even when I first picked her up I could detect the large rust-streaked patches on the hull and see that she was flying the Belgian flag. And the time, shortly before noon, was right. I followed her progress and it seemed to me that she was taking a wider sweep than one or two vessels that had preceded her and was going very close indeed to the buoys that marked the channel: but maybe that was where the deepest water lay.

I followed her progress till she closed on the harbour and then I could distinguish the rather scarred name on the rusty bows. *Marianne* the name read. The captain was certainly a stickler for punctuality, but whether he was such a stickler for abiding by the law was another question.

I went down to the Havenrestaurant and had lunch. I

wasn't hungry but meal-times in Amsterdam, as my experience had been since coming there, tended to be irregular and infrequent. The food in the Havenrestaurant is well spoken of and I've no doubt it merits its reputation: but I don't remember what I had for lunch that day.

I arrived at the Hotel Touring at one-thirty. I didn't really expect to find that Maggie and Belinda had returned yet and they hadn't. I told the man behind the desk that I'd wait in the lounge, but I don't much fancy lounges, especially when I had to study papers like the papers I had to study from the folder we'd taken from Morgenstern and Muggenthaler's, so I waited till the desk was momentarily unmanned, took the lift to the fourth floor and let myself into the girls' room. It was a fractionally better room than the previous one they'd had, and the couch, which I immediately tested, was fractionally softer, but there wasn't enough in it to make Maggie and Belinda turn cartwheels for joy, apart from the fact that the first cartwheel in any direction would have brought them up against a solid wall.

I lay on that couch for over an hour, going through all the warehouse's invoices and a very unexciting and innocuous list of invoices they turned out to be. But there was one name among all the others that turned up with surprising frequency and as its products matched with the line of my developing suspicions, I made a note of its name and map location.

A key turned in the lock and Maggie and Belinda entered. Their first reaction on seeing me seemed to be one of relief, which was quickly followed by an unmistakable air of annoyance. I said mildly: 'Is there something up, then?'

'You had us worried,' Maggie said coldly. 'The man at the desk said you were waiting for us in the lounge and you weren't there.'

'We waited half an hour.' Belinda was almost bitter about it. 'We thought you had gone.'

'I was tired. I had to lie down. Now that I've apologized, how did your morning go?'

'Well—' Maggie didn't seem very mollified—'we had no luck with Astrid—'

'I know. The man at the desk gave me your message. We can quit worrying about Astrid. She's gone.'

'Gone?' they said.

'Skipped the country.'

'Skipped the country?'

'Athens.'

'Athens?'

'Look,' I said. 'Let's keep the vaudeville act for later. She and George left Schiphol this morning.'

'Why?' Belinda asked.

'Scared. The bad men were leaning on her from one side and the good guy—me—on the other. So she lit out.'

'How do you *know* she's gone?' Maggie enquired.

'A man at the Balinova told me.' I didn't elaborate, if they'd any illusions left about the nice boss they had I wanted them to keep them. 'And I checked with the airport.'

'Mm.' Maggie was unimpressed by my morning's work, she seemed to have the feeling that it was all my fault that Astrid had gone and as usual she was right. 'Well, Belinda or me first?'

'This first.' I handed her the paper with the figures 910020 written on it. 'What does it mean?'

Maggie looked at it, turned it upside down and looked at the back. 'Nothing,' she said.

'Let me see it,' Belinda said brightly. 'I'm good at anagrams and cross-words.' She was, too. Almost at once she said: 'Reverse it. 020019. Two a.m. on the 19th, which is tomorrow morning.'

'Not bad at all,' I said indulgently. It had taken me half an hour to work it out.

'What happens then?' Maggie asked suspiciously.

'Whoever wrote those figures forgot to explain that,' I said evasively, for I was getting tired of telling outright lies. 'Well, Maggie, you.'

'Well.' She sat down and smoothed out a lime-green

cotton dress which looked as if it had shrunk an awful lot with repeated washing. 'I put on this new dress to the park because Trudi hadn't seen it before and the wind was blowing so I had a scarf over my head and—'

'And you were wearing dark glasses.'

'Right.' Maggie wasn't an easy girl to throw off stride. 'I wandered around for half an hour, dodging pensioners and prams most of the time. Then I saw her—or rather I saw this enormous fat old—old—'

'Beldam?'

'Beldam. Dressed like you said she would be. Then I saw Trudi. Long-sleeved white cotton dress, couldn't keep still, skipped about like a lamb.' Maggie paused and said reflectively: 'She really is a rather beautiful girl.'

'You have a generous soul, Maggie.'

Maggie took the hint. 'By and by they sat down on a bench. I sat on another about thirty yards away, just looking over the top of a magazine. A Dutch magazine.'

'A nice touch,' I approved.

'Then Trudi started plaiting the hair of this puppet—'

'What puppet?'

'The puppet she was carrying,' Maggie said patiently. 'If you keep on interrupting I find it difficult to remember all the details. While she was doing this a man came up and sat beside them. A big man in a dark suit with a priest's collar, white moustache, marvellous white hair. He seemed a very nice man.'

'I'm sure he was,' I said mechanically. I could well imagine the Rev. Thaddeus Goodbody as a man of instant charm except, perhaps, at half-past three in the morning.

'Trudi seemed very fond of him. After a minute or two, she reached an arm round his neck and whispered something in his ear. He made a great play of being shocked but you could see he wasn't really, for he reached a hand into his pocket and pressed something into her hand. Money, I suppose.' I was on the point of asking if she was sure it wasn't a hypodermic syringe, but Maggie was far too nice for that. 'Then she rose, still clutching this puppet, and skipped across to an ice-cream van. She bought an ice-cream cornet—and then she started walking straight towards me.'

'You left?'

'I held the magazine higher,' Maggie said with dignity. 'I needn't have bothered. She headed past me towards another open van about twenty feet away.'

'To admire the puppets?'

'How did you know?' Maggie sounded disappointed.

'Every second van in Amsterdam seems to sell puppets.'

'That's what she did. Fingered them, stroked them. The old man in charge tried to look angry but who could be angry with a girl like that? She went right round the van, then went back to the bench. She kept on offering the cornet to the puppet.'

'And didn't seem upset when the puppet didn't want any. What were the old girl and the pastor doing the while?'

'Talking. They seemed to have a lot to talk about. Then Trudi got back and they all talked some more, then the pastor patted Trudi on the back, they all rose, he took his hat off to the old girl, as you call her, and they all went away.'

'An idyllic scene. They went away together?'

'No. The pastor went by himself.'

'Try to follow any of them?'

'No.'

'Good girl. Were you followed?'

'I don't think so.'

'You don't think so?'

'There was a whole crowd of people leaving at the same time as I did. Fifty, sixty, I don't know. It would be silly for me to say that I was sure nobody had an eye on me. But nobody followed me back here.'

'Belinda?'

'There's a coffee-shop almost opposite the Hostel Paris. Lots of girls came and went from the hostel but I was on my fourth cup before I recognized one who'd been in the church last night. A tall girl with auburn hair, striking, I suppose you would call her—'

'How do you know what I'd call her? She was dressed like a nun last night.'

'Yes.'

'Then you couldn't have seen that she had auburn hair.'

'She had a mole high up on her left cheekbone.'

'And black eyebrows?' Maggie put in.

'That's her,' Belinda agreed. I gave up. I believed them. When one good-looking girl examines another good-looking girl her eyes are turned into long-range telescopes. 'I followed her to the Kalverstraat,' Belinda continued. 'She went into a big store. She seemed to walk haphazardly through the ground floor but she wasn't being haphazard really for she fetched up pretty quickly at a counter marked "SOUVENIRS: EXPORT ONLY". The girl examined the souvenirs casually but I knew she was far more interested in the puppets than anything else.'

'Well, well, well,' I said. 'Puppets again. How did you know she was interested?'

'I just knew,' Belinda said in the tone of one trying to describe various colours to a person who has been blind from birth. 'Then after a while she started to examine a particular group of puppets very closely. After shilly-shallying for a while she made her choice, but I knew she wasn't shilly-shallying.' I kept prudent silence. 'She spoke to the assistant who wrote something on a piece of paper.'

'The time it would—'

'The time it would take to write the average address.' She'd carried on blandly as if she hadn't heard me. 'Then the girl passed over money and left.'

'You followed her?'

'No. Am I a good girl too?'

'Yes.'

'And I wasn't followed.'

'Or watched? In the store, I mean. By, for instance, any big fat middle-aged man.'

Belinda giggled. 'Lots of big—'

'All right, all right, so lots of big fat middle-aged men spend a lot of time watching you. And lots of young thin

137

ones, too, I shouldn't wonder.' I paused consideringly. 'Tweedledum and Tweedledee, I love you both.'

They exchanged glances. 'Well,' Belinda said, 'that is nice.'

'Professionally speaking, dear girls, professionally speaking. Excellent reports from both, I must say. Belinda, you saw the puppet the girl chose?'

'I'm *paid* to see things,' she said primly.

I eyed her speculatively, but let it go. 'Quite. It was a Huyler costumed puppet. Like the one we saw in the warehouse.'

'How on earth did you know?'

'I could say I'm psychic. I could say "genius". The fact of the matter is that I have access to certain information that you two don't.'

'Well, then, share it with us.' Belinda, of course.

'No.'

'Why not?'

'Because there are men in Amsterdam who could take you and put you in a quiet dark room and make you talk.'

There was a long pause, then Belinda said: 'And you wouldn't?'

'I might at that,' I admitted. 'But they wouldn't find it so easy to get me into that quiet dark room in the first place.' I picked up a batch of the invoices. 'Either of you ever heard of the Kasteel Linden. No? Neither had I. It seems, however, that they supply our friends Morgenstern and Muggenthaler with a large proportion of pendulum clocks.'

'Why pendulum clocks?' Maggie asked.

'I don't know,' I lied frankly. 'There may be a connection. I'd asked Astrid to try to trace the source of a certain type of clock—she had, you understand, a lot of underworld connections that she didn't want. But she's gone now. I'll look into it tomorrow.'

'We'll do it today,' Belinda said. 'We could go to this Kasteel place and—'

'You do that and you're on the next plane back to England. Alternatively, I don't want to waste time dragging you up from the bottom of the moat that surrounds this castle. Clear?'

'Yes, sir,' they said meekly and in unison. It was becoming distressingly and increasingly plain that they didn't regard my bite as being anywhere near as bad as my bark.

I gathered the papers and rose. 'The rest of the day is yours. I'll see you tomorrow morning.'

Oddly, they didn't seem too happy about getting the rest of the day to themselves. Maggie said: 'And you?'

'A car trip to the country. To clear my head. Then sleep, then maybe a boat trip tonight.'

'One of those romantic night cruises on the canals?' Belinda tried to speak lightly but it didn't come off. She and Maggie appeared to be on to something I'd missed. 'You'll need someone to watch your back, won't you? I'll come.'

'Another time. But *don't* you two go out on the canals. *Don't* go near the canals. *Don't* go near the night-clubs. And, above all, *don't* go near the docks or that warehouse.'

'And *don't* you go out tonight either.' I stared at Maggie. Never in five years had she spoken so vehemently, so fiercely even: and she's certainly never told me what to do. She caught my arm, another unheard-of thing. 'Please.'

'Maggie!'

'Do you have to take that boat trip tonight?'

'Now, Maggie—'

'At two o'clock in the morning?'

'What's wrong, Maggie? It's not like you to—'

'I don't know. Yes, I *do* know. Somebody seems to be walking over my grave with hob-nailed boots.'

'Tell him to mind how he goes.'

Belinda took a step towards me. 'Maggie's right. You mustn't go out tonight.' Her face was tight with concern.

'You, too, Belinda?'

'Please.'

There was a strange tension in the room which I couldn't even begin to comprehend. Their faces were pleading, a curious near-desperation in their eyes, much as if I'd just announced that I was going to jump off a cliff.

Belinda said: 'What Maggie means is, don't leave us.'

Maggie nodded. 'Don't go out tonight. Stay with us.'

'Oh, hell!' I said. 'Next time I need help abroad I'm going to bring a couple of big girls with me.' I made to move past them towards the door, but Maggie barred the way, reached up and kissed me. Only seconds later Belinda did the same.

'This is very bad for discipline,' I said. Sherman out of his depth. 'Very bad indeed.'

I opened the door and turned to see if they agreed with me. But they said nothing, just stood there looking curiously forlorn. I shook my head in irritation and left.

On the way back to the Rembrandt I bought brown paper and string. In the hotel room I used this to wrap up a complete kit of clothes that was now more or less recovered from the previous night's soaking, printed a fictitious name and address on it and took it down to the desk. The assistant manager was in position.

'Where's the nearest post office?' I asked.

'My dear Mr Sherman—' The punctiliously friendly greeting was automatic but he'd stopped smiling by this time—'we can attend to that for you.'

'Thank you, but I wish to register it personally.'

'Ah, I understand.' He didn't understand at all, which was that I didn't want brows raised or foreheads creased over the sight of Sherman leaving with a large brown parcel under his arm. He gave me the address I didn't want.

I put the parcel in the boot of the police car and drove through the city and the suburbs until I was out in the country, heading north. By and by I knew I was running alongside the waters of the Zuider Zee but I couldn't see them because of the high retaining dyke to the right of the road. There wasn't much to see on the left hand either: the Dutch countryside is not designed to send the tourist into raptures.

Presently I came to a signpost reading 'Huyler 5 km', and a few hundred yards further on turned left off the road and stopped the car soon after in the tiny square of a tiny picture-postcard village. The square had its post office and outside the post office was a public telephone-box. I locked the boot and doors of the car and left it there.

I made my way back to the main road, crossed it and climbed up the sloping grass-covered dyke until I could look out over the Zuider Zee. A fresh breeze sparkled the waters blue and white under the late afternoon sun, but, scenically, one couldn't say much more for that stretch of water, for the encompassing land was so low that it appeared, when it appeared at all, as no more than a flat dark bar on the horizon. The only distinctive feature anywhere to be seen was an island to the north-east, about a mile off-shore.

This was the island of Huyler and it wasn't even an island. It had been, but some engineers had built a causeway out to it from the mainland to expose the islanders more fully to the benefits of civilization and the tourist trade. Along the top of this causeway a tarmac highway had been laid.

Nor did the island itself even deserve the description of distinctive. It was so low-lying and flat that it seemed that a wave of any size must wash straight over it, but its flatness was relieved by scattered farm-houses, several big Dutch barns and, on the western shore of the island, facing towards the mainland, a village nestling round a tiny harbour. And, of course, it had its canals. That was all there was to be seen, so I left, regained the road, walked along till I came to a bus stop and caught the first bus back to Amsterdam.

I elected for an early dinner, for I did not expect to have much opportunity to eat later that night and I had the suspicion that whatever the fates had in store for me that night had better not be encountered on a full stomach. And then I went to bed, for I didn't anticipate having any sleep later that night either.

The travel alarm awoke me at half-past midnight. I didn't feel particularly rested. I dressed carefully in a dark suit, navy roll-neck jersey, dark rubber-soled canvas shoes and

141

a dark canvas jacket. The gun I wrapped in a zipped oilskin bag and jammed into the shoulder-holster. Two spare magazines went into a similar pouch and I secured those in a zipped pocket of the canvas jacket. I looked longingly at the bottle of Scotch on the side-board and decided against it. I left.

I left, as was by now second nature to me, by the fire-escape. The street below, as usual, was deserted and I knew that nobody followed me as I left the hotel. It wasn't necessary for anyone to follow me for those who wished me ill knew where I was going and where they could expect to find me. I knew they knew. What I hoped was that no one knew that I knew.

I elected to walk because I didn't have the car any more and because I had become allergic to taxis of Amsterdam. The streets were empty, at least the streets I chose were. It seemed a very quiet and peaceful city.

I reached the docks area, located myself, and moved on till I stood in the dark shadow of a storage shed. The luminous dial of my watch told me that it was twenty minutes to two. The wind had increased in strength and the air had turned much colder, but there was no rain about although there was rain in the air. I could smell it over the strong nostalgic odours of sea and tar and ropes and all the other things that make dockside areas smell the same the world over. Tattered dark clouds scudded across the only fractionally less dark sky, occasionally revealing a glimpse of a pale high half-moon, more often obscuring it, but even when the moon was hidden the darkness was never absolute, for above there were always rapidly changing patches of starlit sky.

In the brighter intervals I looked out across the harbour that stretched away into first dimness and then nothingness. There were literally hundreds of barges to be seen in this, one of the great barge harbours of the world, ranging in size from tiny twenty-footers to the massive Rhine barges, all jammed in a seemingly inextricable confusion. The confusion, I knew, was more apparent than real. Close packed the barges undoubtedly were but, although it would call for the most intricate manoeuvring, each barge had, in fact, access to a narrow sea lane, which might intersect with two or three progressively larger lanes before reaching the open water beyond. The barges were connected to land by a series of long wide floating gangways, which in turn had other and narrower gangways attached at right angles to them.

The moon went behind a cloud. I moved out of the shadows on to one of the main central gangways, my rubber shoes quite soundless on the wet wood, and even had I been clumping along in hob-nailed boots I question whether anyone—other than those who were ill-intentioned to me—would have paid any heed, because although all the barges were almost certainly inhabited by their crews and in many cases their crews and families, there were only one or two scattered cabin lights to be seen among all the hundreds of craft lying there: and apart from the faint threnody of the wind and the soft creaking and rubbing as the wind made the barges work gently at their moorings, the silence was total. The barge harbour was a city in itself and the city was asleep.

I'd traversed about a third of the length of the main gangway when the moon broke through. I stopped and looked round.

About fifty yards behind me two men were walking purposefully and silently towards me. They were but shadows, silhouettes, but I could see that the silhouettes of their right arms were longer than those of their left arms. They were carrying something in their right hands. I wasn't surprised to see those objects in their hands just as I hadn't been surprised to see the men themselves.

I glanced briefly to my right. Two more men were advancing steadily from land on the adjacent paralleling gangway to the right. They were abreast with the two on my own gangway.

I glanced to the left. Two more of them, two more moving dark silhouettes. I admired their co-ordination.

I turned and kept on walking towards the harbour. As I went, I extracted the gun from its holster, removed the waterproof covering, zipped up the covering again and replaced it in a zipped pocket. The moon went behind a cloud. I began to run, and as I did so I glanced over my shoulder. The three pairs of men had also broken into a run. I made another five yards and glanced over my shoulder again. The two men on my gangway had stopped and were lining up their guns on me, or seemed to be, because it was difficult to see in the starlight, but a moment later I was convinced they had for narrow red flames licked out in the darkness although there was no sound of shots, which was perfectly understandable for no man in his right senses was going to upset hundreds of tough Dutch, German and Belgian bargees if he could possibly help it. They appeared, however, to have no objection to upsetting me. The moon came out again and I started to run a second time.

The bullet that hit me did more damage to my clothes than it did to me although the swift burning pain on the outside of my upper right arm made me reach up involuntarily to clasp it. Enough was enough. I swerved off the main gangway, jumped on to the bows of a barge that was moored by a small gangway at right angles and ran silently along the deck till I got in the shelter of the wheelhouse aft. Once in shelter, I edged a cautious eye round the corner.

The two men on the central gangway had stopped and were making urgent sweeping motions to their friends on the right, indicating that I should be outflanked and, more likely than not, shot in the back. They had, I thought, very limited ideas about what constituted fair play and sportsmanship: but there was no questioning their efficiency. Quite plainly, if they were going to get me at all—and I rated their chances as good—it was going to be by this encircling or outflanking method and it would obviously be a very good thing for me if I could disabuse them of this idea as soon as I could; so I temporarily ignored the two men on the central gangway, assuming, and correctly, I hoped, that they would remain where they were and wait for the outflankers to catch me unawares, and turned round to face the left gangway.

Five seconds and they were in view, not running, but walking deliberately and peering into the moon-shadows cast by the wheelhouses and cabins of the barges, which was a very foolhardy or just simply foolish thing to do because I was in the deepest shadow I could find while they, by contrast, were almost brutally exposed by the light of the half-moon and I saw them long before they ever saw me. I doubt whether they ever saw me. One of them, for a certainty, did not, for he never saw anything again: he must have been dead before he struck the gangway and slid with a curious absence of noise, no more than a sibilant splash, into the harbour. I lined up for a second shot, but the other man had reacted very quickly indeed and flung himself backwards out of my line of sight before I could squeeze the trigger again. It occurred to me, for no reason at all, that my sportsmanship was on an even lower level than theirs, but I was in the mood for sitting ducks that night.

I turned and moved for'ard again and peered round the edge of the wheelhouse. The two men on the central gangway hadn't moved. Perhaps they didn't know what had happened. They were a very long way away for an accurate pistol shot by night, but I took a long steady careful aim and tried anyway. But this duck was too far away. I heard a man give an exclamation and clutch his leg, but from the alacrity with which he followed his companion and jumped from the gangway into the shelter of a barge he couldn't have been badly hurt. The moon went behind a cloud again, a very small cloud, but the only cloud for the next minute or so and they had me pin-pointed. I scrambled along the barge, regained the main gangway and started to run further out into the harbour.

I hadn't got ten yards when that damned moon made its presence felt again. I flung myself flat, landing so that I faced inshore. To my left the gangway was empty which was hardly surprising as the confidence of the remaining man there must have been badly shaken. I glanced to my right. The two men there were much closer than the two who had just so prudently vacated the central gangway and from the fact that they were still walking forward in a purposeful and confident manner it was apparent that they did not yet know that one of their number was at the bottom of the harbour, but they were as quick to learn the virtue of prudence as the other three had been, for they disappeared from the gangway very quickly when I loosed off two quick and speculative shots at them, both of which clearly missed. The two men who had been on the central gangway were making a cautious attempt to regain it, but they were too far away to worry me or I them.

For another five minutes this deadly game of hide-and-seek went on, running, taking cover, loosing off a shot, then running again, while all the time they closed in inexorably on me. They were being very circumspect now, taking the minimum of chances and using their superior numbers cleverly to advantage, one or two engaging my attention while the others scuttled forward from the shelter of one barge to the next. I was soberly and coldly aware that if I didn't do something different and do it very soon, there could be only one end to this game, and that it must come soon.

Of all the inappropriate times to do so, I chose several of the brief occasions I spent sheltering behind cabins and wheelhouses to think about Belinda and Maggie. Was this, I wondered, why they couldn't see me now, for not only would they have known they had behaved so queerly the last time I had seen them? Had they guessed, or known by some peculiarly feminine intuitive process, that something like this was going to happen to me and known what the end would be and been afraid to tell me? It was as well, I thought, that they had been right but their faith in the infallibiliy of their boss would have been sadly shaken. I felt desperate and I supposed I must have looked pretty much the same way; I'd expected to find a man with a quick gun or a quicker knife lying in wait for me and I

think I could have coped with that, with luck even with
two of them: but I had not expected this. What had I said
to Belinda outside the warehouse?—'He who fights and
runs away lives to fight another day.' But now I had no
place to run to for I was only twenty yards short of the
end of the main gangway. It was a macabre feeling to
be hunted to death like a wild animal or a dog with rabies
while hundreds of people were sleeping within a hundred
yards of me and all I had to do to save myself was to
unscrew my silencer and fire two shots in the air and
within seconds the entire barge harbour would have been in
life-saving uproar. But I couldn't bring myself to do this,
for what I had to do had to be done tonight and I knew this
was the last chance I would ever have. My life in
Amsterdam after tonight wouldn't be worth a crooked
farthing. I couldn't bring myself to do it if there was
left to me even the slenderest chance imaginable. I didn't
think there was, not what a sane man would call a chance.
I don't think I was quite sane then.

I looked at my watch. Six minutes to two. In yet another
way, time had almost run out. I looked at the sky. A small
cloud was drifting towards the moon and this   be the
minute they would choose for the next and almost certainly
last assault: it would have to be the moment I chose for
my next and almost certainly last attempt to escape. I
looked at the deck of the barge: its cargo was scrap and
I picked up a length of metal. I again gauged the direction
of that dark little cloud, which seemed to have grown
even littler. Its centre wasn't going to pass directly across
the moon but it would have to do.

I'd five shots left in my second magazine and I fired them
off in quick succession at where I knew or guessed my
pursuers had taken cover. I hoped this might hold them for
a few seconds but I don't think I really believed it. Quickly
I shoved the gun back in its waterproof covering, zipped it
up and for extra security stowed it not in its holster but in
a zipped pocket of my canvas coat, ran along the barge
for a few steps, stepped on the gunwale and threw myself
on to the main gangway. I scrambled desperately to my

feet and as I did I realized that the damned cloud had missed the moon altogether.

I suddenly felt very calm because there were no options open to me now. I ran, because there was nothing else in the world I could do, weaving madly from side to side to throw my would-be executioners off aim. Half a dozen times in not three seconds I heard soft thudding sounds —they were as close to me as that now—and twice felt hands that I could not see tugging fiercely at my clothes. Suddenly I threw my head back, flung both arms high in the air and sent the piece of metal spinning into the water and had crashed heavily to the gangway even before I heard the splash. I struggled drunkenly and briefly to my feet, clutched my throat, and toppled over backwards into the canal. I took as deep a breath as possible and held it against the impact.

The water was cold, but not icily so, opaque and not very deep. My feet touched mud and I kept them touching mud. I began to exhale, very slowly, very carefully, husbanding my air reserves which probably weren't very much as I didn't go in for this sort of thing very often. Unless I had miscalculated the eagerness of my pursuers to do away with me—and I hadn't—the two men on the central gangway would have been peering hopefully down at the spot where I had disappeared within five seconds of my disappearance. I hoped that they drew all the wrong conclusions from the slow stream of bubbles drifting to the top of the water and I hoped they drew them soon, for I couldn't keep up this kind of performance very much longer.

After what seemed about five minutes but was probably not more than thirty seconds I stopped exhaling and sending bubbles to the surface for the excellent reason that I had no more air left in my lungs to exhale. My lungs were beginning to hurt a little now. I could almost hear my heart—I could certainly feel it—thudding away in an empty chest, and my ears ached. I pushed clear of the mud and swam to my right and hoped to God I'd got myself orientated right. I had. My hand came in contact with the keel of a barge and I used the purchase obtained to pass quickly under, then swam up to the surface.

I don't think I could have stayed below for even a few seconds longer without swallowing water. As it was, when I broke surface it took considerable restraint and will-power to prevent me from drawing in a great lungful of air with a whoop that could have been heard half-way across the harbour, but in certain circumstances, such as when your life depends on it, one can exercise a very considerable amount of will-power indeed and I made do with several large but silent gulps of air.

At first I could see nothing at all, but this was just because of the oily film on the surface of the water that had momentarily glued my eyelids together. I cleared this but still there wasn't much to see, just the dark hull of the barge I was hiding behind, the main gangway in front of me, and another parallel barge about ten feet distant. I could hear voices, a soft murmuring of voices. I swam silently to the stern of the barge, steadied myself by the rudder and peered cautiously round the stern. Two men, one with a torch, were standing on the gangway peering down at the spot where I had so recently disappeared: the waters were satisfactorily dark and still.

The two men straightened. One of them shrugged and made a gesture with the palms of both hands held upwards: the second man nodded agreement and rubbed his leg tenderly. The first man lifted his arms and crossed them above his head twice, first to his left, then to his right. Just as he did so there was a staccato and spluttering coughing sound as a marine diesel, somewhere very close indeed, started up. It was obvious that neither of the two men cared very much for this new development, for the man who had made the signal at once grabbed the arm of the other and led him away, hobbling badly, at the best speed he could muster.

I hauled myself aboard the barge, which sounds a very simple exercise indeed, but when a sheer-sided bull is four feet clear of the water this simple exercise can turn out to be a near-impossibility and so it turned out for me. But

149

I made it eventually with the aid of the stern-rope, flopped over the gunwale and lay there for a full half minute, gasping away like a stranded whale, before a combination of the beginnings of recovery from complete exhaustion and a mounting sense of urgency had me on my feet again and heading towards the barge's bows and the main gangway.

The two men who had been so lately bent on my destruction and were now no doubt full of that righteous glow which comes from the satisfaction of a worthwhile job well done were now no more than two vaguely discerned shadows disappearing into the even deeper shadows of the storage sheds on shore. I pulled myself on to the gangway and crouched there for a moment until I had located the source of the diesel, then stooped, ran quickly along the gangway till I came to the place where the barge was secured to a side gangway, first dropping to my hands and knees, then inching along on knees and elbows before peering over the edge of the gangway.

The barge was at least seventy feet in length, broad in proportion and as totally lacking in grace of design as it was possible to be. The for'ard threequarters of the barge was given up entirely to battened holds, then after that came the wheelhouse and, right aft and joined to the wheelhouse, the crew accommodation. Yellow lights shone through the curtained windows. A large man in a dark peaked cap was leaning out of a wheelhouse window talking to a crew member who was about to clamber on to the side gangway to cast off.

The stern of the barge was hard against the main gangway on which I was lying. I waited till the crew member had climbed on to the side gangway and was walking away to cast off for'ard, then slithered down soundlessly on to the stern of the barge and crouched low behind the cabin until I heard the sound of ropes being thrown aboard and the hollow thump of feet on wood as the man jumped down from the side gangway. I moved silently for'ard until I came to an iron ladder fitted to the fore end of the cabin, climbed up this and edged for'ard in

150

a prone position till I was stretched flat on the stepped wheelhouse roof. The navigation lights came on but this was no worry: they were so positioned on either side of the wheelhouse roof that they had the comforting effect of throwing the position in which I lay into comparatively deeper shadow.

The engine note deepened and the side gangway slowly dropped astern. I wondered bleakly if I had stepped from the frying-pan into the fire.

CHAPTER TEN

I had been pretty certain that I would be putting out to sea that night and anyone who did that under the conditions I expected to experience should also have catered for the possibility of becoming very wet indeed; if I had used even a modicum of forethought in that respect I should have come along fully fitted out with a waterproof scuba suit: but the thought of a waterproof scuba suit had never even crossed my mind and I had no alternative now but to lie where I was and pay the price for my negligence.

I felt as if I were rapidly freezing to death. The night wind out in the Zuider Zee was bitter enough to have chilled even a warmly clad man who was forced to lie motionless, and I wasn't warmly clad. I was soaked to the skin with sea-water and that chilling wind had the effect of making me feel that I had turned into a block of ice—with the difference that a block of ice is inert while I shivered continuously like a man with black-water fever. The only consolation was that I didn't give a damn if it rained: I couldn't possibly become any wetter than I was already.

With numbed and frozen fingers that wouldn't stay steady I unzipped my jacket pockets, took both the gun and the remaining magazine from their waterproof coverings, loaded the gun and stuck it inside my canvas coat. I wondered idly what would happen if, in an emergency, I found that my trigger finger had frozen solid, so I pushed my right hand inside my sodden jacket. The only effect this had was to make my hand feel colder than ever, so I took it out again.

The lights of Amsterdam were dropping far behind now and we were well out into the Zuider Zee. The barge, I noticed, seemed to be following the same widely curving course as the *Marianne* had done when she had come into harbour at noon on the previous day. It passed very close indeed to a couple of buoys and, looking over the bows, it

152

seemed to me as if it was on a collision course with a third buoy about four hundred yards ahead. But I didn't doubt for a minute that the barge skipper knew just exactly what he was doing.

The engine note dropped as the revolutions dropped and two men emerged on deck from the cabin—the first crew to appear outside since we'd cleared the barge harbour. I tried to press myself even closer to the wheelhouse roof, but they didn't come my way, they headed towards the stern. I twisted round the better to observe them.

One of the men carried a metal bar to which was attached a rope at either end. The two men, one on either side of the poop, paid out a little of their lines until the bar must have been very close to water level. I twisted and looked ahead. The barge, moving very slowly now, was no more than twenty yards distant from the flashing buoy and on a course that would take it within twenty feet of it. I heard a sharp word of command from the wheelhouse, looked aft again and saw that the two men were beginning to let the lines slip through their fingers, one man counting as he did so. The reason for the counting was easy to guess. Although I couldn't see any in the gloom, the ropes must have been knotted at regular intervals to enable the two men who were paying them out to keep the iron bar at right angles to the barge's passage through the water.

The barge was exactly abreast the buoy when one of the men called out softly and at once, slowly but steadily, they began to haul their lines inboard. I knew now what was going to happen but I watched pretty closely all the same. As the two men continued to pull, a two-foot cylindrical buoy bobbed clear of the water. This was followed by a four-bladed grapnel, one of the flukes of which was hooked round the metal bar. Attached to this grapnel was a rope. The buoy, grapnel and metal bar were hauled aboard, then the two men began to pull on the grapnel rope until eventually an object came clear of the water and was brought inboard. The object was a grey, metal-banded metal box, about eighteen inches square and twelve deep. It was taken immediately inside the cabin, but even before this

153

was done the barge was under full power again and the buoy beginning to drop rapidly astern. The entire operation had been performed with the ease and surety which bespoke a considerable familiarity with the technique just employed.

Time passed, and a very cold, shivering and miserable time it was too. I thought it was impossible for me to become any colder and wetter than I was but I was wrong, for about four in the morning the sky darkened and it began to rain and I had never felt rain so cold. By this time what little was left of my body heat had managed partially to dry off some of the inner layers of clothing, but from the waist down—the canvas jacket provided reasonable protection—it just proved to have been a waste of time. I hoped that when the time came that I had to move and take to the water again I wouldn't have reached that state of numbed paralysis where all I could do was sink.

The first light of the false dawn was in the sky now and I could vaguely distinguish the blurred outlines of land to the south and east. Then it became darker again and for a time I could see nothing, and then the true dawn began to spread palely from the east and I could see land once more and gradually came to the conclusion that we were fairly close in to the north shore of Huyler and about to curve away to the south-west and then south towards the island's little harbour.

I had never appreciated that those damned barges moved so slowly. As far as the coastline of Huyler was concerned, the barge seemed to be standing still in the water. The last thing I wished to happen was to approach the Huyler shore in broad daylight and give rise to comment on the part of the inevitable ship-watchers as to why a crew member should be so eccentric as to prefer the cold roof of the wheelhouse to the warmth inside. I thought of the warmth inside and put the thought out of my mind.

The sun appeared over the far shore of the Zuider Zee but it was no good to me, it was one of those peculiar suns that were no good at drying out clothes and after a little I was glad to see that it was one of those early-morning suns
154

that promised only to deceive, for it was quickly overspread by a pall of dark cloud and soon that slanting freezing rain was hard at work again, stopping what little circulation I had left. I was glad because the cloud had the effect of darkening the atmosphere again and the rain might persuade the harbour rubber-neckers to stay at home.

We were coming towards journey's end. The rain, now mercifully, had strengthened to the extent where it was beginning to hurt my exposed face and hands and was hissing whitely into the sea: visibility was down to only a couple of hundred yards and although I could see the end of the row of navigation marks towards which the barge was now curving, I couldn't see the harbour beyond.

I wrapped the gun up in its waterproof cover and jammed it in its holster. It would have been safer, as I'd done previously, to have put it in the zipped pocket of my canvas jacket, but I wasn't going to take the canvas jacket with me. At least, not far: I was so numbed and weakened by the long night's experience that the cramping and confining effects of that cumbersome jacket could have made all the difference between my reaching shore or not: another thing I'd carelessly forgotten to take with me was an inflatable life-jacket or belt.

I wriggled out of the canvas jacket and balled it up under my arm. The wind suddenly felt a good deal icier than ever but the time for worrying about that was gone. I slithered along the wheelhouse roof, slid silently down the ladder, crawled below the level of the now uncurtained cabin windows, glanced quickly for'ard—an unnecessary precaution, no one in his right mind would have been out on deck at that moment unless he had to—dropped the canvas jacket overboard, swung across the stern-quarter, lowered myself to the full length of my arms, checked that the screw was well clear of my vicinity, and let go.

It was warmer in the sea than it had been on the wheel-house roof, which was as well for me as I felt myself to be almost frighteningly weak. It had been my intention to tread water until the barge had entered harbour, or at least, under these prevailing conditions, it had disappeared into the murk of the rain, but if ever there was a time for dispensing with refinements this was it. My primary concern, my only concern at the moment, was survival. I ploughed on after the fast receding stern of the barge with the best speed I could muster.

It was a swim, not more than ten minutes in duration, that any six-year-old in good training could have accomplished with ease, but I was way below that standard that morning, and though I can't claim it was a matter of touch and go, I couldn't possibly have done it a second time. When I could clearly see the harbour wall I sheered off from the navigation marks, leaving them to my right, and finally made shore.

I sloshed my way up the beach and, as if by a signal, the rain suddenly stopped. Cautiously, I made my way up the slight eminence of earth before me, the top of which was level with the top of the harbour wall, stretched myself flat on the soaking ground and cautiously lifted my head.

Immediately to the right of me were the two tiny rectangular harbours of Huyler, the outer leading by a narrow passage to the inner. Beyond the inner harbour lay the pretty picture-postcard village of Huyler itself, which, with the exception of the one long and two short straight streets lining the inner harbour itself, was a charming maze of twisting roads and a crazy conglomeration of, mainly, green and white painted houses mounted on stilts as a precaution against flood-water. The stilts were walled in for use as cellars, the entrance to the houses being by outside wooden stairs to the first floor.

I returned my attention to the outer harbour. The barge was berthed alongside its inner wall and the unloading of the cargo was already busily under way. Two small shore derricks lifted a succession of crates and sacks from the unbattened holds, but I had no interest in those crates and sacks, which were certainly perfectly legitimate cargo, but in the small metal box that had been picked up from the sea and which I was equally certain was the most illegi-

timate cargo imaginable. So I let the legitimate cargo look
after itself and concentrated my attention on the cabin
of the barge. I hoped to God I wasn't already too
late, although I could hardly see how I could have been.

I wasn't, but it had been a near thing. Less than thirty
seconds after I had begun my surveillance of the cabin,
two men emerged, one carrying a sack over his shoulder.
Although the sack's contents had clearly been heavily
padded, there was an unmistakable angularity to it that
left me in little doubt that this was the case that interested
me.

The two men went ashore. I watched them for a few
moments to get a general idea of the direction they were
taking, slid back down the muddy bank—another item on
my expense account, my suit had taken a terrible beating
that night—and set off to follow the two men.

They were easy to follow. Not only had they plainly no
suspicion that they were being followed, those narrow and
crazily winding lanes made Huyler a shadow's paradise.
Eventually the two men brought up at a long, low building
on the northern outskirts of the village. The ground floor
—or cellar as it would be in this village—was made of
concrete. The upper storey, reached by a set of wooden
steps similar to another concealing set of steps from which
I was watching at a safe distance of forty yards, had tall
and narrow windows with bars so closely set that a cat
would have had difficulty in penetrating, the heavy door
had two metal bars across it and was secured by two large
padlocks. Both men mounted the stairs, the unburdened
man unlocking the two padlocks and opening the door, then
both passed inside. They reappeared again within twenty
seconds, locked the door behind them and left. Both men
were now unburdened.

I felt a momentary pang of regret that the weight of my
burglar's belt had compelled me to leave it behind that
night, but one does not go swimming with considerable
amounts of metal belted around one's waist. But the regret
was only momentary. Apart from the fact that fifty different
windows overlooked the entrance to this heavily barred

building and the fact that a total stranger would almost certainly be instantly recognizable to any of the villagers in Huyler, it was too soon yet to show my hand: minnows might make fair enough eating but it was the whales I was after and I needed the bait in that box to catch them.

I didn't need a street guide to find my way out of Huyler. The harbour lay to the west, so the terminus of the causeway road must lie to the east. I made my way along a few narrow winding lanes, in no mood to be affected by the quaint old-world charm that drew so many tens of thousands of tourists to the village each summer, and came to a small arched bridge that spanned a narrow canal. The first three people I'd seen in the village so far, three Huyler matrons dressed in their traditional flowing costumes, passed me by as I crossed the bridge. They glanced at me incuriously, then as indifferently looked away again as if it were the most natural thing in the world to meet in the streets of Huyler in the early morning a man who had obviously been recently immersed in the sea.

A few yards beyond the canal lay a surprisingly large car park—at the moment it held only a couple of cars and half a dozen bicycles, none of which had padlock or chain or any other securing device. Theft, apparently, was no problem on the island of Huyler, a fact which I found hardly surprising: when the honest citizens of Huyler went in for crime they went in for it in an altogether bigger way. The car park was devoid of human life nor had I expected to find an attendant at that hour. Feeling guiltier about it than about any other action I had performed since arriving at Schiphol Airport, I selected the most roadworthy of the bicycles, trundled it up to the locked gate, lifted it over, followed myself, and pedalled on my way. There were no cries of 'Stop thief!' or anything of the kind.

It was years since I'd been on a bicycle, and though I was in no fit state to recapture that first fine careless rapture I got the hang of it again quickly enough, and while I hardly enjoyed the trip it was at least better than walking and had
158

the effect of getting some of my red corpuscles on the move again.

I parked the bicycle in the tiny village square where I'd left the police taxi—it was still there—and looked thoughtfully first at the telephone-box, then at my watch: I decided it was still too early, so I unlocked the car and drove off.

Half a mile along the Amsterdam road I came to an old Dutch barn standing well apart from its farm-house. I stopped the car on the road in such a position that the barn came between it and anyone who might chance to look out from the farm-house. I unlocked the boot, took out the brown paper parcel, made for the barn, found it unlocked, went inside and changed into a completely dry set of clothing. It didn't have the effect of transforming me into a new man, I still found it impossible to stop shivering, but at least I wasn't sunk in the depths of that clammily ice-cold misery that I'd been in for hours past.

I went on my way again. After only another half-mile I came to a roadside building about the size of a small bungalow whose sign defiantly claimed that it was a motel. Motel or not, it was open, and I wanted no more. The plump proprietress asked if I wanted breakfast, but I indicated that I had other and more urgent needs. They have in Holland the charming practice of filling your glass of *jonge Genever* right to the very brim and the proprietress watched in astonishment and considerable apprehension as my shaking hands tried to convey the liquid to my mouth. I didn't lose more than half of it in spillage, but I could see she was considering calling either police or medical aid to cope with an alcoholic with the DT's or a drug addict who had lost his hypodermic, whichever the case might be, but she was a brave woman and supplied me with my second *jonge Genever* on demand. This time I didn't lose more than a quarter of it, and third time round not only did I spill hardly a drop but I could distinctly feel the rest of my layabout red corpuscles picking up their legs and giving themselves a brisk workout. With the fourth *jonge Genever* my hand was steady as a rock.

I borrowed an electric razor, then had a gargantuan breakfast of eggs and meat and ham and cheeses, about four different kinds of bread and half a gallon, as near as dammit, of coffee. The food was superb. Fledgling motel it might have been, but it was going places. I asked to use the phone.

I got through to the Hotel Touring in seconds, which was a great deal less time than it took for the desk to get any reply from Maggie's and Belinda's room. Finally, a very sleepy-voiced Maggie said: 'Hullo. Who is it?' I could just see her standing there, stretching and yawning.

'Out on the tiles last night, eh?' I said severely.

'What?' She still wasn't with me.

'Sound asleep in the middle of the day.' It was coming up for eight a.m. 'Nothing but a couple of mini-skirted layabouts.'

'Is it—is it *you*?'

'Who else but the lord and master?' The *jonge Genevers* were beginning to make their delayed effect felt.

'Belinda! He's back!' A pause. 'Lord and master, he says.'

'I'm so glad!' Belinda's voice. 'I'm so glad. We—'

'You're not half as glad as I am. You can get back to your bed. Try to beat the milkman to it tomorrow morning.'

'We didn't leave our room.' She sounded very subdued. 'We talked and worried and hardly slept a wink and we thought—'

'I'm sorry. Maggie? Get dressed. Forget about the foam baths and breakfast. Get—'

'No breakfast? I'll bet you had breakfast.' Belinda was having a bad influence on this girl.

'I had.'

'And stayed the night in a luxury hotel?'

'Rank hath its privileges. Get a taxi, drop it on the outskirts of the town, phone for a local taxi and come out towards Huyler.'

'Where they make the puppets?'

'That's it. You'll meet me coming south in a yellow and

160

red taxi.' I gave her the registration number. 'Have your driver stop. Be as fast as you can.'

I hung up, paid up and went on my way. I was glad I was alive. Glad to be alive. It had been the sort of night that didn't look like having any morning, but here I was and I was glad. The girls were glad. I was warm and dry and fed, the *jonge Genever* was happily chasing the red corpuscles in a game of merry-go-round, all the coloured threads were weaving themselves into a beautiful pattern and by day's end it would be over. I had never felt so good before.

I was never to feel so good again.

Nearing the suburbs I was flagged down by a yellow taxi. I stopped and crossed the road just as Maggie got out. She was dressed in a navy skirt and jacket and white blouse and if she'd spent a sleepless night she certainly showed no signs of it. She looked beautiful, but then she always looked that way: there was something special about her that morning.

'Well, well, well,' she said. 'What a healthy-looking ghost. May I kiss you?'

'Certaintly not,' I said with dignity. 'Relationships between employer and employed are—'

'Do be quiet, Paul.' She kissed me without permission. 'What do you want me to do?'

'Go out to Huyler. Plenty of places down by the harbour where you can get breakfast. There's a place I want you to keep under fairly close but not constant surveillance.' I described the window-barred building and its location. 'Just try to see who goes in and out of that building and what goes on there. And remember, you're a tourist. Stay in company or as close as you can to company all the time. Belinda's still in her room?'

'Yes.' Maggie smiled. 'Belinda took a phone call while I was dressing. Good news, I think.'

'Who does Belinda know in Amsterdam?' I said sharply. 'Who called?'

'Astrid Lemay.'

'What in God's name are you talking about? Astrid's skipped the country. I've got proof.'

'Sure she skipped it.' Maggie was enjoying herself. 'She skipped it because you'd given her a very important job to do and she couldn't do it because she was being followed everywhere she went. So she skipped out, got off at Paris, got a refund on her Athens ticket and skipped straight back in again. She and George are staying in a place outside Amsterdam with friends she can trust. She says to tell you she followed that lead you gave her. She says to tell you she's been out to the Kasteel Linden and that—'

'Oh my God!' I said. 'Oh my God!' I looked at Maggie standing there, the smile slowly dying on her lips and for one brief moment I felt like turning savagely on her, for her ignorance, for her stupidity, for her smiling face, for her empty talk of good news, and then I felt more ashamed of myself than I had ever done in my life, for the fault was mine, not Maggie's, and I would have cut off my hand sooner than hurt her, so instead I put my arm round her shoulders and said: 'Maggie, I must leave you.'

She smiled at me uncertainly. 'I'm sorry. I don't understand.'

'Maggie?'

'Yes, Paul?'

'How do you think Astrid Lemay found out the telephone number of your new hotel?'

'Oh, dear God!' she said, for now she understood.

I ran across to my car without looking back, started up and accelerated through the gears like a man possessed, which I suppose I really was. I operated the switch that popped up the blue flashing police light and turned on the siren, then clamped the earphones over my head and started fiddling desperately with the radio control knobs. Nobody had ever shown me how to work it and this was hardly the time to learn. The car was full of noise, the high-pitched howling of the over-stressed engine, the clamour of the siren, the static and crackle of the earphones and, what seemed loudest of all to me, the sound of my harsh and bitter and futile swearing as I tried to get that damned radio to work. Then suddenly the crackling ceased and I heard a calm assured voice.

'Police headquarters,' I shouted. 'Colonel de Graaf. Never mind who the hell I am. Hurry, man, hurry!' There was a long and infuriating silence as I weaved through the morning rush-hour traffic and then a voice on the earphones said: 'Colonel de Graaf is not in his office yet.'

'Then get him at home!' I shouted. Eventually they got him at home. 'Colonel de Graaf? Yes, yes, yes. Never mind that. That puppet we saw yesterday. I *have* seen a girl like that before. Astrid Lemay.' De Graaf started to ask questions but I cut him short. 'For God's sake, never mind that. The warehouse—I think she's in desperate danger. We're dealing with a criminal maniac. For God's sake, hurry.'

I threw the earphones down and concentrated on driving and cursing myself. If you want a candidate for easy out-witting, I thought savagely, Sherman's your man. But at the same time I was conscious that I was being at least a degree unfair to myself: I was up against a brilliantly directed criminal organization, that was for sure, but an organization that contained within it an unpredictable psychopathic element that made normal prediction almost impossible. Sure, Astrid had sold Jimmy Duclos down the river, but it had been Duclos or George, and George was a brother. They'd sent her to get to work on me, for she herself could have had no means of knowing that I was staying at the Rembrandt, but instead of enlisting my aid and sympathy she'd chickened out at the last moment and I'd had her traced and that was when the trouble had begun, that was when she had begun to become a liability instead of an asset. She had begun seeing me—or I her —without their ostensible knowledge. I could have been seen taking George away from that barrel-organ in the Rembrandtplein or at the church or by those two drunks outside her flat who weren't drunks at all.

They'd eventually decided that it was better to have her out of the way, but not in such a fashion that would make me think that harm had come to her because they probably thought, and rightly, that if I thought she'd been taken prisoner and was otherwise in danger I'd have abandoned all hope of achieving my ultimate objective and done what they knew now was the very last thing I wanted to do —go to the police and lay before them all I knew, which they probably suspected was a great deal. This, too, was the last thing they wanted me to do because although by going to the police I would have defeated my own ultimate ends, I could so severely damage their organization that it might take months, perhaps years, to build it up again. And so Durrell and Marcel had played their part yesterday morning in the Balinova while I had overplayed mine to the hilt and had convinced me beyond doubt that Astrid and George had left for Athens. Sure they had. They'd left all right, been forced off the plane at Paris and forced to return to Amsterdam. When she'd spoken to Belinda, she'd done so with a gun at her head.

And now, of course, Astrid was no longer of any use to them. Astrid had gone over to the enemy and there was only one thing to do with people like that. And now, of course, they need no longer fear any reaction from me, for I had died at two o'clock that morning down in the barge harbour. I had the key to it all now, because I knew why they had been waiting. But I knew the key was too late to save Astrid.

I hit nothing and killed no one driving through Amsterdam, but that was only because its citizens have very quick reactions. I was in the old town now, nearing the warehouse and travelling at high speed down the narrow one-way street leading to it when I saw the police barricade, a police car across the street with an armed policeman at either end of it. I skidded to a halt. I jumped out of the car and a policeman approached me.

'Police,' he said, in case I thought he was an insurance salesman or something. 'Please go back.'

'Don't you recognize one of your own cars?' I snarled. 'Get out of my damned way.'

'No one is allowed into this street.'

'It's all right.' De Graaf appeared round the corner and

164

if I hadn't known from the police car the expression on his face would have told me. 'It's not a very pleasant sight, Major Sherman.'

I walked past him without speaking, rounded the corner and looked upwards. From this distance the puppet-like figure swinging lazily from the hoisting beam at the top of Morgenstern and Muggenthaler's warehouse looked hardly larger than the puppet I had seen yesterday morning, but then I had seen that one from directly underneath, so this one had to be bigger, much bigger. It was dressed in the same traditional costume as had been the puppet that had swayed to and fro there only so short a time ago: I didn't have to get any closer to know that the puppet's face of yesterday would be a perfect replica of the face that was there now. I turned away and walked round the corner, de Graaf with me.

'Why don't you take her down?' I asked. I could hear my own voice coming as if from a distance, abnormally, icily calm and quite toneless.

'It's a job for a doctor. He's gone up there now.'

'Of course.' I paused and said: 'She can't have been there long. She was alive less than an hour ago. Surely the warehouse was open long before—'

'This is Saturday. They don't work on Saturdays.'

'Of course,' I repeated mechanically. Another thought had come into my head, a thought that struck an even deeper fear and chill into me. Astrid, with a gun at her head, had phoned the Touring. But she had phoned with a message for me, and that message had been meaningless and could or should have achieved nothing, for I was lying at the bottom of the harbour. It could only have had a purpose if the message had been relayed to me. It would have only been made if they knew I was still alive. How could they have known I was still alive? Who could have conveyed the information that I was still alive? Nobody had seen me—except the three matrons on Huyler. And why should they concern themselves—

There was more. Why should they make her telephone me and then put themselves and their plans in jeopardy by

165

killing Astrid after having been at such pains to convince me that she was alive and well? Suddenly, certainly, I knew the answer. They had forgotten something. I'd forgotten something. They forgot what Maggie had forgotten, that Astrid did not know the telephone number of their new hotel: and I'd forgotten that neither Maggie nor Belinda had ever met Astrid or heard her speak. I walked back round the corner. Below the gable of the warehouse the chain and hook still stirred slightly: but the burden was gone.

I said to de Graaf: 'Get the doctor.' He appeared in two minutes, a youngster, I should have thought, fresh out of medical school and looking paler, I suspected, than he normally did.

I said harshly: 'She's been dead for hours, hasn't she?'

He nodded. 'Four, five, I can't be sure.'

'Thank you.' I walked away back round the corner, de Graaf accompanying me. His face held a score of unasked questions, but I didn't feel like answering any of them.

'I killed her,' I said. 'I think I may have killed someone else, too.'

'I don't understand,' de Graaf said.

'I think I have sent Maggie to die.'

'Maggie?'

'I'm sorry. I didn't tell you. I had two girls with me, both from Interpol. Maggie was one of them. The other is at the Hotel Touring.' I gave him Belinda's name and telephone number. 'Contact her for me, will you, please? Tell her to lock her door and stay there till she hears from me and that she is to ignore any phone or written message that does not contain the word "Birmingham". Will you do it personally, please?'

'Of course.'

I nodded at de Graaf's car. 'Can you get through on the radio telephone to Huyler?'

He shook his head.

'Then police headquarters, please.' As de Graaf spoke to

his driver, a grim-faced van Gelder came round the corner. He had a handbag with him.

'Astrid Lemay's?' I asked. He nodded. 'Give it to me, please.'

He shook his head firmly. 'I can't do that. In a case of murder—'

'Give it to him,' de Graaf said.

'Thank you,' I said to de Graaf: 'Five feet four, long black hair, blue eyes, very good-looking, navy skirt and jacket, white blouse and white handbag. She'll be in the area—'

'One moment.' De Graaf leaned towards his driver, then said: 'The lines to Huyler appear to be dead. Death does seem to follow you around, Major Sherman.'

'I'll call you later this morning,' I said, and turned for my car.

'I'll come with you,' van Gelder said.

'You have your hands full here. Where I'm going I don't want any policemen.'

Van Gelder nodded. 'Which means you are going to step outside the law.'

'I'm already outside the law. Astrid Lemay is dead. Jimmy Duclos is dead. Maggie may be dead. I want to talk to people who make other people dead.'

'I think you should give us your gun,' van Gelder said soberly.

'What do you expect me to have in my hands when I talk to them? A Bible? To pray for their souls? First you kill me, van Gelder, then you take away the gun.'

De Graaf said: 'You have information and you are withholding it from us?'

'Yes.'

'This is not courteous, wise or legal.'

I got into my car. 'As for the wisdom, you can judge later. Courtesy and legality no longer concern me.'

I started the engine and as I did van Gelder made a move towards me and I heard de Graaf saying: 'Leave him be, Inspector, leave him be.'

CHAPTER ELEVEN

I didn't make many friends on the way back out to Huyler but then I wasn't in the mood for making friends. Under normal circumstances, driving in the crazy and wholly irresponsible way I did, I should have been involved in at least half a dozen accidents, all of them serious, but I found that the flashing police light and siren had a near-magical effect of clearing the way in front of me. At a distance up to half a mile approaching vehicles or vehicles going in the same direction as I was would slow down or stop, pulling very closely in to the side of the road. I was briefly pursued by a police car that should have known better, but the police driver lacked my urgency of motivation and he was clearly and sensibly of the opinion that there was no point in killing himself just to earn his weekly wage. There would be, I knew, an immediate radio alert, but I had no fear of road blocks or any such form of molestation: once the licence plate number was received at HQ I'd be left alone.

I would have preferred to complete the journey in another car or by bus, for one quality in which a yellow and red taxi is conspicuously lacking is unobtrusiveness, but haste was more important than discretion. I compromised by driving along the final stretch of the causeway at a comparatively sedate pace: the spectacle of a yellow and red taxi approaching the village at speed of something in the region of a hundred miles an hour would have given rise to some speculation even among the renownedly incurious Dutch.

I parked the car in the already rapidly filling car park, removed my jacket, shoulder-holster and tie, upended my collar, rolled up my sleeves, and emerged from the car with my jacket hung carelessly over my left arm: under the jacket I carried my gun with the silencer in place.

The notoriously fickle Dutch weather had changed
168

dramatically for the better. Even as I had left Amsterdam
the skies had been clearing and now there were only drifting
cotton-wool puffs in an otherwise cloudless sky and the
already hot sun was drawing up steam from the houses
and adjoining fields. I walked leisurely but not too leisurely
towards the building I'd asked Maggie to keep under observation. The door stood wide open now and at intervals
I could see people, all women in their traditional costumes,
moving around the interior: occasionally one emerged and
went into the village, occasionally a man came out with a
carton which he would place on a wheelbarrow and trundle
into the village. This was the home of a cottage industry
of some sort: what kind of industry was impossible to judge
from the outside. That it appeared to be an entirely innocuous industry was evidenced by the fact that tourists
who occasionally happened by were smilingly invited to
come inside and look around. All the ones I saw go inside
came out again, so clearly it was the least sinister of places.
North of the building stretched an almost unbroken expanse
of hayfields and in the distance I could see a group of
traditionally dressed matrons tossing hay in the air to dry it
off in the morning sun. The men of Huyler, I reflected,
seemed to have it made: none of them appeared to do any
work at all.

There was no sign of Maggie. I wandered back into the
village, bought a pair of tinted spectacles—heavy dark
spectacles instead of acting as an aid to concealment tend
to attract attention, which is probably why so many people
wear them—and a floppy straw hat that I wouldn't have
been seen dead in outside Huyler. It was hardly what
one could call a perfect disguise, for nothing short of stain
could ever conceal the white scars on my face, but at least
it helped to provide me with a certain degree of anonymity
and I didn't think I looked all that different from scores of
other tourists wandering about the village.

Huyler was a very small village, but when you start looking for someone concerning whose whereabouts you have
no idea at all and when that someone may be wandering
around at the same time as you are, then even the smallest

169

village can become embarrassingly large. As briskly as I could without attracting attention, I covered every lane in Huyler and saw no trace of Maggie.

I was in a pretty fair way towards quiet desperation now, ignoring the voice in my mind that told me with numbing certainty that I was too late, and feeling all the more frustrated by the fact that I had to conduct my search with at least a modicum of leisure. I now started on a tour of all the shops and cafés although, if Maggie were still alive and well, I hardly expected to find her in any of those in view of the assignment I had given her. But I couldn't afford to ignore any possibility

The shops and cafés round the inner harbour yielded nothing—and I covered every one of them. I then moved out in a series of expanding concentric circles, as far as one can assign so geometrical a term in the maze of haphazard lanes that was Huyler. And it was on the outermost of these circles that I found Maggie, finding her alive, well and totally unscathed: my relief was hardly greater than my sense of foolishness.

I found her where I should have thought to find her right away if I had been using my head as she had been. I'd told her to keep the building under surveillance but at the same time to keep in company and she was doing just that. She was inside a large crowded souvenir shop, fingering some of the articles for sale, but not really looking at them: she was looking fixedly, instead, at the large building less than thirty yards away, so fixedly, that she quite failed to notice me. I took a step to go inside the door to speak to her when I suddenly saw something that held me quite still and made me look as fixedly as Maggie was, although not in the same direction.

Trudi and Herta were coming down the street. Trudi, dressed in a sleeveless pink frock and wearing long white cotton gloves, skipped along in her customary childish fashion, her blonde hair swinging, a smile on her face: Herta, clad in her usual outlandish dress, waddled gravely alongside, carrying a large leather bag in her hand.

I didn't stand on the order of my going. I stepped quickly

inside the shop: but not in Maggie's direction, whatever else happened I didn't want those two to see me talking to her: instead I took up a strategic position behind a tall revolving stand of picture-postcards and waited for Herta and Trudi to pass by.

They didn't pass by. They passed by the front door, sure enough, but that was as far as they got, for Trudi suddenly stopped, peered through the window where Maggie was standing and caught Herta by the arms. Seconds later she coaxed the plainly reluctant Herta inside the shop, took her arm away from Herta who remained hovering there broodingly like a volcano about to erupt, stepped forward and caught Maggie by the arm.

'I know you,' Trudi said delightedly. 'I know you!'

Maggie turned and smiled. 'I know you too. Hullo, Trudi.'

'And this is Herta.' Trudi turned to Herta, who clearly approved of nothing that was taking place. 'Herta, this is my friend, Maggie.'

Herta scowled in acknowledgment.

Trudi said: 'Major Sherman is my friend.'

'I know that,' Maggie smiled.

'Are you my friend, Maggie?'

'Of course I am, Trudi.'

Trudi seemed delighted. 'I have lots of other friends. Would you like to see them?' She almost dragged Maggie to the door and pointed. She was pointing to the north and I knew it could be only at the haymakers at the far end of the field. 'Look. There they are.'

'I'm sure they're very nice friends,' Maggie said politely.

A picture-postcard hunter edged close to me, as much as to indicate that I should move over and let him have a look: I'm not quite sure what kind of look I gave him but it certainly was sufficient to make him move away very hurriedly.

'They are *lovely* friends,' Trudi was saying. She nodded at Herta and indicated the bag she was carrying. 'When Herta and I come here we always take them out food and coffee in the morning.' She said impulsively: 'Come and see

171

them, Maggie,' and when Maggie hesitated said anxiously: 'You *are* my friend, aren't you?'

'Of course, but—'

'They are such nice friends,' Trudi said pleadingly. 'They are so happy. They make music. If we are very good, they may do the hay dance for us.'

'The hay dance?'

'Yes, Maggie. The hay dance. Please, Maggie. You are all my friends. Please come. Just for me, Maggie?'

'Oh, very well.' Maggie was laughingly reluctant. 'Just for you, Trudi. But I can't stay long.'

'I *do* like you, Maggie.' Trudi squeezed Maggie's arm. 'I do like you.'

The three of them left. I waited a discreet period of time, then moved cautiously out of the shop. They were already fifty yards away, past the building I'd asked Maggie to watch and out into the hayfield. The haymakers were at least six hundred yards away, building their first haystack of the day close in to what looked, even at that distance, to be a pretty ancient and decrepit Dutch barn. I could hear the chatter of voices as the three of them moved out over the stubbled hay and all the chatter appeared to come from Trudi, who was back at her usual gambit of gambolling like a spring lamb. Trudi never walked: she always skipped.

I followed, but not skipping. A hedgerow ran alongside the edge of the field and I prudently kept this between myself and Herta and the two girls, trailing thirty or forty yards behind. I've no doubt that my method of locomotion looked almost as peculiar as Trudi's because the hedgerow was less than five feet in height and I spent most of the six hundred yards bent forward at the hips like a septuagenarian suffering from a bout of lumbago.

By and by the three of them reached the old barn and sat down on the west side, in the shadow from the steadily strengthening sun. I got the barn between them and the haymakers on the one hand and myself on the other, ran quickly across the intervening space and let myself in by a side door.

I hadn't been wrong about the barn. It must have been at least a century old and appeared to be in a very dilapidated condition indeed. The floor-boards sagged, the wooden walls bulged at just about every point where they could bulge and some of the original air-filtering cracks between the horizontal planks had warped and widened to the extent that one could almost put one's head through them.

There was a loft to the barn, the floor of which appeared to be in imminent danger of collapse: it was rotted and splintered and riddled with woodworm; even an English house-agent would have had difficulty in disposing of the place on the basis of its antiquity. It didn't look as if it could support an averagely-built mouse, far less my weight, but the lower part of the barn was of little use for observation, and besides, I didn't want to peer out of one of those cracks in the wall and find someone else peering in about two inches away, so I reluctantly took the crumbling flight of wooden steps that led up to the loft.

The loft, the east side of which was still half full of last year's hay, was every bit as dangerous as it looked but I picked my steps with caution and approached the west side of the barn. This part of the barn had an even better selection of gaps between the planks and I eventually located the ideal one, at least six inches in width and affording an excellent view. I could see the heads of Maggie, Trudi and Herta directly beneath: I could see the matrons, about a dozen in all, assiduously and expertly building a haystack, the tines of their long-handled hayforks gleaming in the sun: I could even see part of the village itself, including most of the car park. I had a feeling of unease and could not understand the reason for this: the haymaking scene taking place out on the field there was as idyllic as even the most bucolic-minded could have wished to see. I think the odd sense of apprehension sprang from the least unlikely source, the actual haymakers themselves, for not even here, in their native setting, did those flowing striped robes, those exquisitely embroidered dresses and snowy wimple hats appear quite natural. There

173

was a more than faintly theatrical quality about them, an aura of unreality. I had the feeling, almost, that I was witnessing a play being staged for my benefit.

About half an hour passed during which the matrons worked away steadily and the three sitting beneath me engaged in only desultory conversation: it was that kind of day, warm and still and peaceful, the only sounds being the swish of the hayforks and the distant murmuring of bees, that seems to make conversation of any kind unnecessary. I wondered if I dared risk a cigarette and decided I dared: I fumbled in the pocket of my jacket for matches and cigarettes, laid my coat on the floor with the silenced gun on top of it, and lit the cigarette, careful not to let any of the smoke escape through the gaps in the planks.

By and by Herta consulted a wristwatch about the size of a kitchen alarm clock and said something to Trudi, who rose, reached down a hand and pulled Maggie to her feet. Together they walked towards the haymakers, presumably to summon them to their morning break, for Herta was spreading a chequered cloth on the ground and laying out cups and unwrapping food from folded napkins.

A voice behind me said: 'Don't try to reach for your gun. If you do, you'll never live to touch it.'

I believed the voice. I didn't try to reach for my gun.

'Turn round very slowly.'

I turned round very slowly. It was that kind of voice.

'Move three paces away from the gun. To your left.'

I couldn't see anyone. But I heard him all right. I moved three paces away. To the left.

There was a stirring in the hay on the other side of the loft and two figures emerged: the Reverend Thaddeus Goodbody and Marcel, the snakelike dandy I'd clobbered and shoved in the safe in the Balinova. Goodbody didn't have a gun in his hand, but then, he didn't need one: the blunderbuss Marcel carried in his was as big as two ordinary guns and, to judge from the gleam in the flat black unwinking eyes, he was busily searching for the remotest thread of an excuse to use it. Nor was I encouraged by the fact that his gun had a silencer to it: this meant that they

174

didn't care how often they shot me, nobody would hear a thing.

'Most damnably hot in there,' Goodbody said complainingly. 'And ticklish.' He smiled in that fashion that made little children want to take him by the hand. 'Your calling leads you into the most unexpected places, I must say, my dear Sherman.'

'My calling?'

'Last time I met you, you were, if I remember correctly, purporting to be a taxi-driver.'

'Ah, that time. I'll bet you didn't report me to the police after all.'

'I did have second thoughts about it,' Goodbody conceded generously. He walked across to where my gun lay and picked it up distastefully before throwing it into the hay. 'Crude, unpleasant weapons.'

'Yes, indeed,' I agreed. 'You now prefer to introduce an element of refinement into your killing.'

'As I am shortly about to demonstrate.' Goodbody wasn't bothering to lower his voice but he didn't have to, the Huyler matrons were at their morning coffee now and even with their mouths full they all appeared capable of talking at once. Goodbody walked across to the hay, unearthed a canvas bag and produced a length of rope. 'Be on the alert, my dear Marcel. If Mr Sherman makes the slightest move, however harmless it may seem, shoot him. Not to kill. Through the thigh.'

Marcel licked his lips. I hoped he wouldn't consider the movement of my shirt, caused by the accelerated pumping of my heart, as one that could be suspiciously interpreted. Goodbody approached circumspectly from the rear, tied the rope firmly round my right wrist, passed the rope over a rafter and then, after what seemed an unnecessarily lengthy period of readjustment, secured the rope round my left wrist. My hands were held at the level of my ears. Goodbody brought out another length of rope.

'From my friend Marcel here,' Goodbody said conversationally, 'I have learned that you have a certain expertise with your hands. It occurs to me that you might be similarly

175

gifted with your feet.' He stooped and fastened my ankles together with an enthusiasm that boded ill for the circulation of my feet. 'It further occurs to me that you might have comment to make on the scene you are about to witness. We would prefer to do without the comment.' He stuffed a far from clean handkerchief into my mouth and bound it in position with another one. 'Satisfactory, Marcel, you would say?'

Marcel's eyes gleamed. 'I have a message to deliver to Sherman from Mr Durrell.'

'Now, now, my dear fellow, not so precipitate. Later, later. For the moment, we want our friend to be in full possession of his faculties, eyesight undimmed, hearing unimpaired, the mind at its keenest to appreciate all the artistic nuances of the entertainment we have arranged for his benefit.'

'Of course, Mr Goodbody,' Marcel said obediently. He was back at his revolting lip-licking. 'But afterwards—'

'Afterwards,' Goodbody said generously, 'you may deliver as many messages as you like. But remember—I want him still alive when the barn burns down tonight. It is a pity that we shall be unable to witness it from close quarters.' He looked genuinely sad. 'You and that charming young lady out there—when they find your charred remains among the embers—well, I'm sure they'll draw their own conclusions about love's careless young dream. Smoking in barns, as you have just done, is a most unwise practice. Most unwise. Goodbye, Mr Sherman, and I do not mean au revoir. I think I must observe the hay dance from closer range. *Such* a charming old custom. I think you will agree.'

He left, leaving Marcel to his lip-licking. I didn't much fancy being left alone with Marcel, but that was hardly of any importance in my mind at that moment. I twisted and looked through the gap in the planking.

The matrons had finished their coffee and were lumbering to their feet. Trudi and Maggie were directly beneath where I was standing.

'Were the cakes not nice, Maggie?' Trudi asked. 'And the coffee?'

'Lovely, Trudi, lovely. But I have been too long away. I have shopping to do. I must go now.' Maggie paused and looked up. 'What's that?'

Two piano accordions had begun to play, softly, gently. I could see neither of the musicians: the sound appeared to come from the far side of the haystack the matrons had just finished building.

Trudi jumped to her feet, clapping her hands excitedly. She reached down and pulled Maggie to hers.

'It's the hay dance!' Trudi cried, a child having her birthday treat. 'The hay dance! They are going to do the hay dance! They must like you too, Maggie. They do it for you! You are their friend now.'

The matrons, all of them middle-aged or older, with faces curiously, almost frighteningly lacking in expression, began to move with a sort of ponderous precision. Shouldering their hayforks like rifles, they formed a straight line and began to clump heavily to and fro, their beribboned pigtails swinging as the music from the accordions swelled in volume. They pirouetted gravely, then resumed their rhythmic marching to and fro. The straight line, I saw, was now gradually curving into the shape of a half moon.

'I've never seen a dance like this before.' Maggie's voice was puzzled. I'd never seen a dance like it either and I knew with a sick and chilling certainty that I would never want to see one again—not, it seemed now, that I would ever have the chance to see one again.

Trudi echoed my thoughts, but their sinister implication escaped Maggie.

'And you will never see a dance like this again, Maggie,' she said. 'They are only starting. Oh, Maggie, they must like you—see, they want you!'

'Me?'

'Yes, Maggie. They like you. Sometimes they ask me. Today, you.'

'I must go, Trudi.'

'Please, Maggie. For a moment. You don't do anything. You just stand facing them. *Please*, Maggie. They will be hurt if you don't do this.'

Maggie laughed protestingly, resignedly. 'Oh, very well.'

Seconds later a reluctant and very embarrassed Maggie was standing at the focal point as a semi-circle of hayfork-bearing matrons advanced and retreated towards and from her. Gradually the pattern and the tempo of the dance changed and quickened as the dancers now formed a complete circle about Maggie. The circle contracted and expanded, contracted and expanded, the women bowing gravely as they approached most closely to Maggie, then flinging their heads and pigtails back as they stamped away again.

Goodbody came into my line of view, his smile gently amused and kindly as he participated vicariously in the pleasure of the charming old dance taking place before him. He stood beside Trudi, and put a hand on her shoulder: she smiled delightedly up at him.

I felt I was going to be sick. I wanted to look away, but to look away would have been an abandonment of Maggie and I could never abandon Maggie: but God only knew that I could never help her now. There was embarrassment in her face, now, and puzzlement: and more than a hint of uneasiness. She looked anxiously at Trudi through a gap between two of the matrons: Trudi smiled widely and waved in gay encouragement.

Suddenly the accordion music changed. What had been a gently lilting dance tune, albeit with a military beat to it, increased rapidly in volume as it changed into something of a different nature altogether, something that went beyond the merely martial, something that was harsh and primitive and savage and violent. The matrons, having reached their fully expanded circle, were beginning to close in again. From my elevation I could still see Maggie, her eyes wide now and fear showing in her face: she leaned to one side to look almost desperately for Trudi. But there was no salvation in Trudi: her smile had gone now, her cotton-clad hands were clasped tightly together and she was

178

licking her lips slowly, obscenely. I turned to look at Marcel, who was busy doing the same thing: but he still had his gun on me, and watched me as closely as he watched the scene outside. There was nothing I could do.

The matrons were now stamping their way inwards. Their moonlike faces had lost their expressionless quality and were now pitiless, implacable, and the deepening fear in Maggie's eyes gave way to terror, her eyes staring as the music became more powerful, more discordant still. Then abruptly, with military precision, the shoulder-borne pitchforks were brought sweeping down until they were pointed directly at Maggie. She screamed and screamed again but the sound she made was barely audible above the almost insanely discordant crescendo of the accordions. And then Maggie was down and, mercifully, all I could see was the back view of the matrons as their forks time and again jerked high and stabbed down convulsively at something that now lay motionless on the ground. For the space of a few moments I could look no longer. I had to look away, and there was Trudi, her hands opening and closing, her mesmerized entranced face with a hideous animal-like quality to it: and beside her the Reverend Goodbody, his face as benign and gently benevolent as ever, an expression that belied his staring eyes. Evil minds, sick minds, that had long since left the borders of sanity far behind.

I forced myself to look back again as the music slowly subsided, losing its primeval atavistic quality. The frenzied activities of the matrons had subsided, the stabbing had ceased, and as I watched one of the matrons turned aside and picked up a forkful of hay. I had a momentary glimpse of a crumpled figure with a white blouse no longer white lying on the stubble, then a forkful of hay covered her from sight. Then came another forkful and another and another, and as the two accordions, soft and gentle and muted now, spoke nostalgically of old Vienna, they built a haystack over Maggie. Dr Goodbody and Trudi, she again smiling and chattering gaily, walked off arm in arm towards the village.

Marcel turned away from the gap in the planks and

179

sighed. 'Dr Goodbody manages those things so well, don't you think? The flair, the sensitivity, the time, the place, the atmosphere—exquisitely done, exquisitely done.' The beautifully modulated Oxbridge accent emanating from that snake's head was no less repellent than the context in which the words were used: he was like the rest of them, quite mad.

He approached me circumspectly from the back, undid the handkerchief which had been tied round my head and plucked out the filthy lump of cotton that had been shoved into my mouth. I didn't think that he was being motivated by any humanitarian considerations, and he wasn't. He said offhandedly: 'When you scream, I want to hear it. I don't think the ladies out there will pay too much attention.'

I was sure they wouldn't. I said: 'I'm suprised Dr Goodbody could drag himself away.' My voice didn't sound like any voice I'd ever used before: it was hoarse and thick and I'd difficulty in forming the words as if I'd damaged my larynx.

Marcel smiled. 'Dr Goodbody has urgent things to attend to in Amsterdam. Important things.'

'And important things to transport from here to Amsterdam.'

'Doubtless.' He smiled again and I could almost see his hood distending. 'Classically, my dear Sherman, when a person is in your position and has lost out and is about to die, it is customary for a person in my position to explain, in loving detail, just where the victim went wrong. But apart from the fact that your list of blunders is so long as to be too tedious to ennumerate, I simply can't be bothered. So let's get on with it, shall we?'

'Get on with what?' Here it comes now, I thought, but I didn't much care: it didn't seem to matter much any more.

'The message from Mr Durrell, of course.' Pain sliced like a butcher's cleaver through my head and the side of my face as he slashed the barrel of his gun across it. I thought my left cheekbone must be broken, but couldn't be sure: but my tongue told me that two at least of my teeth had been loosened beyond repair.

'Mr Durrell,' Marcel said happily, 'told me to tell you that he doesn't like being pistol-whipped.' He went for the right side of my face this time, and although I saw and knew it was coming and tried to jerk my head back I couldn't get out of the way. This one didn't hurt so badly, but I knew I was badly hurt from the temporary loss of vision that followed the brilliant white light that seemed to explode just in front of my eyes. My face was on fire, my head was coming apart, but my mind was strangely clear. Very little more of this systematic clubbing, I knew, and even a plastic surgeon would shake his head regretfully: but what really mattered was that with very little more of this treatment I would lose consciousness, perhaps for hours. There seemed to be only one hope: to make his clubbing unsystematic.

I spat out a tooth and said: 'Pansy.'

For some reason this got him. The veneer of civilized urbanity couldn't have been thicker than an onion skin to begin with and it just didn't slough off, it vanished in an instant of time and what was left was a mindless beserker savage who attacked me with the wanton, unreasoning and insensate fury of the mentally unhinged, which he almost certainly was. Blows rained from all directions on my head and shoulders, blows from his gun and blows from his fists and when I tried to protect myself as best I could with my forearms he switched his insane assault to my body. I moaned, my eyes turned up, my legs turned to jelly and I would have collapsed had I been in a position to: as it was, I just hung limply from the rope securing my wrists.

Two or three more agony-filled seconds elapsed before he recovered himself sufficiently to realize that he was wasting his time: from Marcel's point of view there could be little point in inflicting punishment on a person who was beyond feeling the effects of it. He made a strange noise in his throat which probably indicated disappointment more than anything else, then just stood there breathing heavily.

What he was contemplating doing next I couldn't guess for I didn't dare open my eyes.

I heard him move away a little and risked a quick glance from the corner of my eye. The momentary madness was over and Marcel, who was obviously as opportunistic as he was sadistic, had picked up my jacket and was going through it hopefully but unsuccessfully, for wallets carried in the inner breast pocket of a jacket invariably fall out when that jacket is carried over the arm and I'd prudently transferred my wallet with its money, passport and driving licence to my hip pocket. Marcel wasn't long in arriving at the right conclusion for almost immediately I heard his footsteps and felt the wallet being removed from my hip pocket.

He was standing by my side now. I couldn't see him, but I was aware of this. I moaned and swung helplessly at the end of the rope that secured me to the rafter. My legs were trailed out behind me, the upper parts of the toes of my shoes resting on the floor. I opened my eyes, just a fraction.

I could see his feet, not more than a yard from where I was. I glanced up, for the fleeting part of a second. Marcel, with an air of concentration and pleased surprise was engrossed in the task of transferring the very considerable sums of money I carried in my wallet to his own pocket. He held the wallet in his left hand, while his gun dangled by the trigger-guard from the crooked middle finger of the same hand. He was so absorbed that he didn't see my hands reach up to get a better purchase on the securing ropes.

I jack-knifed my body convulsively forward and upwards with all the hate and the fury and the pain that was in me and I do not think that Marcel ever saw my scything feet coming. He made no sound at all, just jack-knifed forward in turn as convulsively as I had done, fell against me and slithered slowly to the floor. He lay there and his head rolled from side to side whether in unconscious reflex or in the conscious reflex of a body otherwise numbed in a paroxysm of agony I could not say but I was in no way disposed to take chances. I stood upright, took a long step back as far as my bonds would permit and came at him again. I was vaguely surprised that his head still stayed on his shoulders: it wasn't pretty but then I wasn't dealing with pretty people.

The gun was still hooked round the middle finger of his left hand. I pulled it off with the toes of my shoes. I tried to get a purchase on the gun between my shoes but the friction coefficient between the metal and the leather was too low and the gun kept sliding free. I removed my shoes by dragging the heels against the floor and then, a much longer process, my socks by using the same technique. I abraded a fair amount of skin and collected my quota of wooden splinters in so doing, but was conscious of no real sensation of hurt: the pain in my face made other minor irritation insignificant to the point of non-existence.

My bare feet gave me an excellent purchase on the gun. Keeping them tightly clamped together I brought both ends of the rope together and hauled myself up till I reached the rafter. This gave me four feet of slack rope to play with, more than enough. I hung by my left hand, reached down with my right while I doubled up my legs. And then I had the gun in my hand.

I lowered myself to the floor, held the rope pinioning my left wrist taut and placed the muzzle of the gun against it. The first shot severed it as neatly as any knife could have done. I untied all the knots securing me, ripped off the front of Marcel's snow-white shirt to wipe my bloodied face and mouth, retrieved my wallet and money and left. I didn't know whether Marcel was alive or dead, he looked very dead to me but I wasn't interested enough to investigate.

CHAPTER TWELVE

It was early afternoon when I got back to Amsterdam and the sun that had looked down on Maggie's death that morning had symbolically gone into hiding. Heavy dark cloud rolled in from the Zuider Zee. I could have reached the city an hour earlier than I did, but the doctor in the out-patients department of the suburban hospital where I'd stopped by to have my face fixed had been full of questions and annoyed at my insistence that sticking-plaster—a large amount of it, admittedly—was all I required at the moment and that the stitching and the swathes of white bandaging could wait until later. What with the plaster and assorted bruises and a half-closed left eye I must have looked like the sole survivor from an express train crash, but at least I wasn't bad enough to send young children screaming for their mothers.

I parked the police taxi not far from a hire-garage where I managed to persuade the owner to let me have a small black Opel. He wasn't very keen, as my face was enough to give rise in anyone's mind to doubts about my past driving record, but he let me have it in the end. The first drops of rain were beginning to fall as I drove off, stopped by the police car, picked up Astrid's handbag and two pairs of handcuffs for luck, and went on my way.

I parked the car in what was by now becoming a rather familiar side-street to me and walked down towards the canal. I poked my head around the corner and as hastily withdrew it again: next time I looked I merely edged an eye round.

A black Mercedes was parked by the door of the Church of the American Huguenot Society. Its capacious boot was open and two men were lifting an obviously very heavy box inside: there were already two or three similar boxes deeper inside the boot. One of the men was instantly identifiable as the Reverend Goodbody: the other man,

184

thin, of medium height, clad in a dark suit and with dark hair and a very swarthy face, was as instantly recognizable: the dark and violent man who had gunned down Jimmy Duclos in Schiphol Airport. For a moment or two I forgot about the pain in my face. I wasn't positively happy at seeing this man again but I was far from dejected as he had seldom been very far from my thoughts. The wheel, I felt, was coming full circle.

They staggered out from the church with one more box, stowed it away and closed the boot. I headed back for my Opel and by the time I'd brought it down to the canal Goodbody and the dark man were already a hundred yards away in the Mercedes. I followed at a discreet distance.

The rain was falling in earnest now as the black Mercedes headed west and south across the city. Though not yet mid-afternoon, the sky was as thunderously overcast as if dusk, still some hours away, was falling. I didn't mind, it made for the easiest of shadowing: in Holland it is required that you switch your lights on in heavy rain, and in those conditions one car looked very like the dark shapeless mass of the next.

We cleared the last of the suburbs and headed out into the country. There was no wild element of pursuit or chase about our progress. Goodbody, though driving a powerful car, was proceeding at a very sedate pace indeed, hardly surprising, perhaps, in view of the very considerable weight he was carrying in the boot. I was watching road signs closely and soon I was in no doubt as to where we were heading: I never really had been.

I thought it wiser to arrive at our mutual destination before Goodbody and the dark man did, so I closed up till I was less than twenty yards behind the Mercedes. I had no worry about being recognized by Goodbody in his driving mirror for he was throwing up so dense a cloud of spray that all he could possibly have seen following him was a pair of dipped headlamps. I waited till I could see ahead what seemed to be a straight stretch of road, pulled out and accelerated past the Mercedes. As I drew level Goodbody glanced briefly and incuriously at the car that was overtaking him, then looked as incuriously away again. His face had been no more than a pale blur to me and the rain was so heavy and the spray thrown up by both cars so blinding that I knew it was impossible that he could have recognized me. I pulled ahead and got into the right-hand lane again, not slackening speed.

Three kilometres further on I came to a right-hand fork which read 'Kasteel Linden 1 km'. I turned down this and a minute later passed an imposing stone archway with the words 'Kasteel Linden' engraved in gilt above it. I carried on for perhaps another two hundred yards, then turned off the road and parked the Opel in a deep thicket.

I was going to get very wet again but I didn't seem to have much in the way of options. I left the car and ran across some thinly wooded grassland till I came to a thick belt of pines that obviously served as some kind of windbreak for a habitation. I made my way through the pines, very circumspectly, and there was the habitation all right: the Kasteel Linden. Oblivious of the rain beating down on my unprotected back, I stretched out in the concealment of long grass and some bushes and studied the place.

Immediately before me stretched a circular gravelled driveway which led off to my right to the archway I'd just passed. Beyond the gravel lay the Kasteel Linden itself, a rectangular four-storeyed building, windowed on the first two stories, embrasured above, with the top turreted and crenellated in the best medieval fashion. Encircling the castle was a continuous moat fifteen feet in width and, according to the guide-book, almost as deep. All that was lacking was a drawbridge, although the chain pulleys for it were still to be seen firmly embedded in the thick masonry of the walls: instead, a flight of about twenty wide and shallow stone steps spanned the moat and led to a pair of massive closed doors, which seemed to be made of oak. To my left, about thirty yards distant from the castle, was a rectangular, one-storeyed building in brick and obviously of fairly recent construction.

The black Mercedes appeared through the gateway, crunched its way on to the gravel and pulled up close to the rectangular building. While Goodbody remained inside the car, the dark man got out and made a complete circuit of the castle: Goodbody never had struck me as the kind of man to take chances. Goodbody got out and together the two men carried the contents of the boot into the building: the door had been locked but obviously Goodbody had the right key for it and not a skeleton either. As they carried the last of the boxes inside the door closed behind them.

I rose cautiously to my feet and moved around behind the bushes until I came to the side of the building. Just as cautiously I approached the Mercedes and looked inside. But there was nothing worthy of remark there—not what I was looking for anyway. With an even greater degree of caution I tip-toed up to a side window of the building and peered inside.

The interior was clearly a combination of workshop, store and display shop. The walls were hung with old-fashioned —or replicas of old-fashioned—pendulum clocks of every conceivable shape, size and design. Other clocks and a very large assortment of parts of other clocks lay on four large work-tables, in the process of manufacture or reassembly or reconstruction. At the far end of the room lay several wooden boxes similar to the ones that Goodbody and the dark man had just carried inside: those boxes appeared to be packed with straw. Shelves above those boxes held a variety of other clocks each having lying beside it its own pendulum, chain and weights.

Goodbody and the dark man were working beside those shelves. As I watched, they delved into one of the open boxes and proceeded to bring out a series of pendulum weights. Goodbody paused, produced a paper and proceeded to study it intently. After some time Goodbody pointed at some item on this paper and said something to the dark man, who nodded and went on with his work: Goodbody, still studying the paper as he went, passed through a side door and disappeared from sight. The dark man studied another paper and began arranging pairs of identical weights beside each other.

I was beginning to wonder where Goodbody had got to when I found out. His voice came from directly behind me.

'I *am* glad you haven't disappointed me, Mr Sherman.'

I turned round slowly. Predictably, he was smiling his saintly smile and, equally predictably, he had a large gun in his hand.

'No one is indestructible, of course,' he beamed, 'but you do have a certain quality of resilience, I must confess. It is difficult to underestimate policemen, but I may have been rather negligent in your case. Twice in this one day I had thought I had got rid of your presence, which, I must admit was becoming something of an embarrassment to me. However, I'm sure third time, for me, will prove lucky. You should have killed Marcel, you know.'

'I didn't?'

'Come, come, you must learn to mask your feelings and not let your disappointment show through. He recovered for a brief moment but long enough to attract the attention of the good ladies in the field. But I fear he has a fractured skull and some brain haemorrhage. He may not survive.' He looked at me thoughtfully. 'But he appears to have given a good account of himself.'

'A fight to the death,' I agreed. 'Must we stand in the rain?'

'Indeed not.' He ushered me into the building at the point of his gun. The dark man looked around with no great surprise: I wondered how long had elapsed since they had the warning message from Huyler.

'Jacques,' Goodbody said. 'This is Mr Sherman—*Major* Sherman. I believe he is connected with Interpol or some other such futile organization.'

'We've met,' Jacques grinned.

'Of course. How forgetful of me.' Goodbody pointed his gun at me while Jacques took mine away.

'Just the one,' he reported. He raked the sights across my

cheek, tearing some of the plaster away, and grinned again 'I'll bet that hurts, eh?'

'Restrain yourself, Jacques, restrain yourself,' Goodbody admonished. He had his kindly side to him; if he'd been a cannibal he'd probably have knocked you over the head before boiling you alive. 'Point his gun at him, will you?' He put his own away. 'I must say I never did care for those weapons. Crude, noisy, lacking a certain delicacy—'

'Like hanging a girl from a hook?' I asked. 'Or stabbing one to death with pitchforks.'

'Come, come, let us not distress ourselves.' He sighed. 'Even the best of you people are so clumsy, so obvious. I had, I must confess, expected rather more from you. You, my dear fellow, have a reputation which you've totally failed to live up to. You blunder around. You upset people. fondly imagining you are provoking reactions in the process. You let yourself be seen in all the wrong places. Twice you go to Miss Lemay's flat without taking precautions. You rifle pockets of pieces of paper that were put there for you to discover, and there was no need,' he added reproachfully, 'to kill the waiter in the process. You walk through Huyler in broad daylight—every person in Huyler, my dear Sherman, is a member of my flock. You even left your calling card in the basement of my church the night before last—blood. Not that I bear you any ill-will for that, my dear fellow—I was in fact contemplating getting rid of Henri, who had become rather a liability to me, and you solved the problem rather neatly. And what do you think of our unique arrangements here —those are all reproductions for sale . . .'

'My God,' I said. 'No wonder the churches are empty.'

'Ah! But one *must* savour those moments, don't you think? Those weights there. We measure and weigh them and return at suitable times with replacement weights—like those we brought tonight. Not that our weights *are* quite the same. They have something inside them. Then they're boxed, Customs inspected, sealed and sent on with official

Government approval to certain—friends—abroad. One of my better schemes, I always maintain.'

Jacques cleared his throat deferentially. 'You said you were in a hurry, Mr Goodbody.'

'Ever the pragmatist, Jacques, ever the pragmatist. But you're right, of course. First we attend to our—ah—ace investigator, then to business. See if the coast is clear.'

Goodbody distastefully produced his pistol again while Jacques made a quiet reconnaissance. He returned in a few moments, nodding, and they made me precede them out of the door, across the gravel and up the steps over the moat to the massive oaken door. Goodbody produced a key of the right size to open the door and we passed inside. We went up a flight of stairs, along a passage and into a room.

It was a very big room indeed, almost literally festooned with hundreds of clocks. I'd never seen so many clocks in one place and certainly, I knew, never so valuable a collection of clocks. All, without exception, were pendulum clocks, some of a very great size, all of great age. Only a very few of them appeared to be working, but, even so, their collective noise was barely below the level of toleration. I couldn't have worked in that room for ten minutes.

'One of the finest collections in the world,' Goodbody said proudly as if it belonged to him, 'if not the finest. And as you shall see—or hear—they *all* work.'

I heard his words but they didn't register. I was staring at the floor, at the man lying there with the long black hair reaching down to the nape of his neck, at the thin shoulder-blades protruding through the threadbare jacket. Lying beside him were some pieces of single-core rubber-insulated electrical cable. Close to his head lay a pair of sorbo-rubber-covered earphones.

I didn't have to be a doctor to know that George Lemay was dead.

'An accident,' Goodbody said regretfully, 'a genuine accident. We did not mean it to happen like this. I fear the poor fellow's system must have been greatly weakened by the privations he has suffered over the years.'

'You killed him,' I said.

'Technically, in a manner of speaking, yes.'

'Why?'

'Because his high-principled sister—who has erroneously believed for years that we have evidence leading to the proof of her brother's guilt as a murderer—finally prevailed upon him to go to the police. So we had to remove them from the Amsterdam scene temporarily—but not, of course, in such a way as to upset you. I'm afraid, Mr Sherman, that you must hold yourself partly to blame for the poor lad's death. And for that of his sister. And for that of your lovely assistant—Maggie, I think her name was.' He broke off and retreated hastily, holding his pistol at arm's length. 'Do not throw yourself on my gun. I take it you did not enjoy the entertainment? Neither, I'm sure, did Maggie. And neither, I'm afraid, will your other friend Belinda, who must die this evening. Ah! That strikes deep, I see. You would like to kill me, Mr Sherman.' He was smiling still, but the flat staring eyes were the eyes of a madman.

'Yes,' I said tonelessly, 'I'd like to kill you.'

'We have sent her a little note.' Goodbody was enjoying himself immensely. 'Code word "Birmingham", I believe . . . She is to meet you at the warehouse of our good friends Morgenstern and Muggenthaler, who will now be above suspicion for ever. Who but the insane would ever contemplate perpetrating *two* such hideous crimes on their own premises? So fitting, don't you think? Another puppet on a chain. Like all the thousands of other puppets throughout the world—hooked and dancing to our tune.'

I said: 'You know, of course, that you are quite mad?'

'Tie him up,' Goodbody said harshly. His urbanity had cracked at last. The truth must have hurt him.

Jacques bound my wrists with the thick rubber-covered flex. He did the same for my ankles, pushed me to one side of the room and attached my wrists by another length of rubber cable to an eyebolt on the wall.

'Start the clocks!' Goodbody ordered. Obediently,

Jacques set off around the room starting the pendulums to swing: significantly, he didn't bother about the smaller clocks.

'They all work and they all chime, some most loudly,' Goodbody said with satisfaction. He was back on balance again, urbane and unctuous as ever. 'Those earphones will amplify the sound about ten times. There is the amplifier there and the microphone there, both, as you can see, well beyond your reach. The earphones are unbreakable. In fifteen minutes you will be insane, in thirty minutes unconscious. The resulting coma lasts from eight to ten hours. You will wake up still insane. But you won't wake up. Already beginning to tick and chime quite loudly, aren't they?'

'This is how George died, of course. And you will watch it all happen. Through the top of that glass door, of course. Where it won't be so noisy.'

'Regrettably, not all. Jacques and I have some business matters to attend to. But we'll be back for the most interesting part, won't we, Jacques?'

'Yes, Mr Goodbody,' said Jacques, still industriously swinging pendulums.

'If I disappear—'

'Ah, but you won't. I had intended to have you disappear last night in the harbour but that was crude, a panic measure lacking the hallmark of my professionalism. I have come up with a much better idea, haven't I, Jacques?'

'Yes, indeed, Mr Goodbody.' Jacques had now almost to shout to make himself heard.

'The point is you're not going to disappear, Mr Sherman. Oh, dear me, no. You'll be found, instead, only a few minutes after you've drowned.'

'Drowned?'

'Precisely. Ah, you think, then the authorities will immediately suspect foul play. An autopsy. And the first thing they see are forearms riddled with injection punctures —I have a system that can make two-hour-old punctures look two months old. They will proceed further and find you full of dope—as you will be. Injected when you are

192

unconscious about two hours before we push you, in your car, into a canal, then call the police. This they will not believe. Sherman, the intrepid Interpol narcotics investigator? Then they go through your luggage. Hypodermics, needles, heroin, in your pockets traces of cannabis. Sad, sad. Who would have thought it? Just another of those who hunted with the hounds and ran with the hare.'

'I'll say this much for you,' I said, 'you're a clever madman.'

He smiled, which probably meant he couldn't hear me above the increasing clamour of the clocks. He clamped the sorbo-rubber earphones to my head and secured them immovably in position with literally yards of Scotch tape. Momentarily the room became almost hushed—the earphones were acting as temporary sound insulators. Goodbody crossed the room towards the amplifier, smiled at me again and pulled a switch.

I felt as if I had been subjected to some violent physical blow or a severe electrical shock. My whole body arched and twisted in convulsive jerks and I knew what little could be seen of my face under the plaster and Scotch tape must be convulsed in agony. For I was in agony, an agony a dozen times more piercing and unbearable than the best —or the worst—that Marcel had been able to inflict upon me. My ears, my entire head, were filled with this insanely shrieking banshee cacophony of sound. It sliced through my head like white-hot skewers, it seemed to be tearing my brain apart. I couldn't understand why my eardrums didn't shatter. I had always heard and believed that a loud enough explosion of sound, set off close enough to your ears, can deafen you immediately and for life: but it wasn't working in my case. As it obviously hadn't worked in George's case. In my torment I vaguely remembered Goodbody attributing George's death to his weakened physical condition.

I rolled from side to side, an instinctive animal reaction to escape from what is hurting you, but I couldn't roll far, Jacques had used a fairly short length of rubber cable to secure me to the eyebolt and I could roll no more than a couple of feet in either direction. At the end of one roll I

193

managed to focus my eyes long enough to see Goodbody and Jacques, now both outside the room, peering at
me with interest through the glass-topped door: after a
few seconds Jacques raised his left wrist and tapped his
watch. Goodbody nodded in reluctant agreement and
both men hurried away. I supposed in my blinding sea of
pain that they were in a hurry to come back to witness the
grand finale.

Fifteen minutes before I was unconscious, Goodbody had
said. I didn't believe a word of it, nobody could stand up to
this for two or three minutes without being broken both
mentally and physically. I twisted violently from side to
side, tried to smash the earphones on the floor or to tear
them free. But Goodbody had been right, the earphones
were unbreakable and the Scotch tape had been so skilfully
and tightly applied that my efforts to tear the phones free
resulted only in reopening the wounds on my face.

The pendulums swung, the clocks ticked, the chimes rang
out almost continuously. There was no relief, no let-up, not
even the most momentary respite from this murderous
assault on the nervous system that triggered off those uncontrollable epileptic convulsions. It was one continuous
electric shock at just below the lethal level and I could
now all too easily give credence to tales I had heard of
patients undergoing electric shock therapy who had eventually ended up on the operating table for the repair of
limbs fractured through involuntary muscular contraction.

I could feel my mind going, and for a brief period I tried
to help the feeling along. Oblivion, anything for oblivion.
I'd failed, I'd failed all along the line, everything I'd
touched had turned to destruction and death. Maggie was
dead, Duclos was dead, Astrid was dead and her brother
George. Only Belinda was left and she was going to die that
night. A grand slam.

And then I knew. I knew I couldn't let Belinda die. That
was what saved me, I knew I could not let her die. Pride no
longer concerned me, my failure no longer concerned
me, the total victory of Goodbody and his evil associates
194

was of no concern to me. They could flood the world with their damned narcotics for all I cared. But I couldn't let Belinda die.

Somehow I pushed myself up till my back was against the wall. Apart from the frequent convulsions, I was vibrating in every limb in my body, not just shaking like a man with the ague, that would have been easily tolerated but vibrating as a man would have been had he been tied to a giant pneumatic drill. I could no longer focus for more than a second or two, but I did my best to look fuzzily, desperately around to see if there was anything that offered any hope of salvation. There was nothing. Then, without warning, the sound in my head abruptly rose to a shattering crescendo—it was probably a big clock near the microphones striking the hour—and I fell sideways as if I'd been hit on the temple by a two-by-four. As my head struck the floor it also struck some projection low down on the skirting board.

My focusing powers were now entirely gone, but I could vaguely distinguish objects not less than a few inches away and this one was no more than three. It says much for my now almost completely incapacitated mind that it took me several seconds to realize what it was, but when I did I forced myself into a sitting position again. The object was an electrical wall-socket.

My hands were bound behind my back and it took me for ever to locate and take hold of the two free ends of the electrical cable that held me prisoner. I touched their ends with my fingertips: the wire core was exposed in both cases. Desperately, I tried to force the ends into the sockets —it never occurred to me that it might have been a shuttered plug, although it would have been unlikely in so old a house as this—but my hands shook so much that I couldn't locate them. I could feel consciousness slipping away. I could feel the damned plug, I could feel the sockets with my fingertips, but I couldn't match the ends of the wire with the holes. I couldn't see any more, I had hardly any feeling left in my fingers, the pain was beyond human tolerance and I think I was screaming soundlessly in my agony when suddenly there was a brilliant bluish-white flash and I fell sideways to the floor.

How long I lay there unconscious I could not later tell: it must have been at least a matter of minutes. The first thing I was aware of was the incredible glorious silence, not a total silence, for I could still hear the chiming of clocks, but a muffled chiming only for I had blown the right power fuse and the earphones were again acting as insulators. I sat up till I was in a half-reclining position. I could feel blood trickling down my chin and was to find later that I'd bitten through my lower lip: my face was bathed in sweat, my entire body felt as if it had been on the rack. I didn't mind any of it, I was conscious of only one thing: the utter blissfulness of silence. Those lads in the Noise Abatement Society knew what they were about.

The effects of this savage punishment passed off more swiftly than I would have expected, but far from completely: that pain in my head and eardrums and the overall soreness of my body would be with me for quite a long time to come—that I knew. But the effects weren't wearing off quite as quickly as I thought, because it took me over a minute to realize that if Goodbody and Jacques came back that moment and found me sitting against the wall with what was unquestionably an idiotic expression of bliss on my face, they wouldn't be indulging in any half measures next time round. I glanced quickly up at the glass-topped door but there were no raised eyebrows in sight yet.

I stretched out on the floor again and resumed my rolling to and fro. I was hardly more than ten seconds too soon, for on my third or fourth roll towards the door I saw Goodbody and Jacques thrust their heads into view. I stepped up my performance, rolled about more violently than ever, arched my body and flung myself so convulsively to and fro that I was suffering almost as much as I had been when I was undergoing the real thing. Every time I rolled towards the door I let them see my contorted face, my eyes either staring wide or screwed tightly shut in agony and I think that my sweat-sheened face and the blood welling from my lip and from one or two of the reopened gashes that Marcel had given must have added up to a fairly convincing spectacle. Goodbody and Jacques were both smiling broadly, although Jacques's expression came nowhere near Goodbody's benign saintliness.

I gave one particularly impressive leap that carried my entire body clear of the ground and as I near as a toucher dislocated my shoulder as I landed I decided that enough was enough—I doubt if even Goodbody really knew the par for the course—and allowed my strugglings and writhings to become feebler and feebler until eventually, after one last convulsive jerk, I lay still.

Goodbody and Jacques entered. Goodbody strode across to switch off the amplifier, smiled beautifully and switched it on again: he had forgotten that his intention was not only to render me unconscious but insane. Jacques, however, said something to him, and Goodbody nodded reluctantly and switched off the amplifier again—perhaps Jacques, activated not by compassion but the thought that it might make it difficult for them if I were to die before they injected the drugs, had pointed this out—while Jacques went around stopping the pendulums of the biggest clocks. Then both came across to examine me. Jacques kicked me experimentally in the ribs but I'd been through too much to react to that.

'Now, now, my dear fellow—' I could faintly hear Goodbody's reproachful voice—'I approve your sentiments but no marks, no marks. The police wouldn't like it.'

'But look at his face,' Jacques protested.

'That's so,' Goodbody agreed amicably. 'Anyway, cut his wrists free—wouldn't do to have gouge marks showing on them when the fire brigade fish him out of the canal and remove those earphones and hide them.' Jacques did both in the space of ten seconds: when he removed the earphones it felt as if my face was coming with it: Jacques had a very cavalier attitude towards Scotch tape.

'As for him—' Goodbody nodded at George Lemay —'dispose of him. You know how. I'll send Marcel out to help you bring Sherman in.' There was silence for a few moments. I knew he was looking down at me, then Goodbody sighed. 'Ah, me. Ah, me. Life is but a walking shadow.'

With that, Goodbody took himself off. He was humming as he went, and as far as one can hum soulfully, Goodbody was giving as soulful a rendition of 'Abide with me' as ever I had heard. He had a sense of occasion, had the Reverend Goodbody.

Jacques went to a box in the corner of the room, produced half a dozen large pendulum weights and proceeded to thread a piece of rubber cable through their eyelits and attach the cable to George's waist: Jacques was leaving little doubt as to what he had in mind. He dragged George from the room out into the corridor and I could hear the sound of the dead man's heels rubbing along the floor as Jacques dragged him to the front of the castle. I rose, flexed my hands experimentally, and followed.

As I neared the doorway I could hear the sound of the Mercedes starting up and getting under way. I looked round the corner. Jacques, with George lying on the floor beside him, had the window open and was giving a sketchy salute: it could only have been to the departing Goodbody.

Jacques turned from the window to attend to George's last rites. Instead he stood there motionless, his face frozen in total shock. I was only five feet from him and I could tell even from his stunned lack of expression that he could tell from mine that he had reached the end of his murderous road. Frantically, he scrabbled for the gun under his arm, but for what may well have been the first and was certainly the last time in his life Jacques was too slow, for that moment of paralysed incredulity had been his undoing. I hit him just beneath the ribs as his gun came clear and when he doubled forward wrested the gun from his almost unresisting hand and struck him savagely with it across the temple. Jacques, unconscious on his feet, took one involuntary step back, the window-sill caught him behind the legs and he began to topple outwards and backwards in oddly slow motion. I just stood there and watched him go, and when I heard the splash and only then, I went to the window and looked out. The roiled waters of the moat were rippling against the bank and the castle walls and from the middle of the moat a stream of bubbles ascended. I looked to the left and could see Goodbody's Mercedes rounding the entrance arch to the castle. By this time, I thought, he should have been well into the fourth verse of 'Abide with me'.

I withdrew from the window and walked downstairs. I went out, leaving the door open behind me. I paused briefly on the steps over the moat and looked down, and as I did the bubbles from the bottom of the moat gradually became fewer and smaller and finally ceased altogether.

CHAPTER THIRTEEN

I sat in the Opel, looked at my gun which I'd recovered from Jacques, and pondered. If there was one thing that I had discovered about that gun it was that people seemed to be able to take it from me whenever they felt so inclined. It was a chastening thought but one that carried with it the inescapable conclusion that what I needed was another gun, a second gun, so I brought up Astrid's handbag from under the seat and took out the little Lilliput I had given her. I lifted my left trouser-leg a few inches, thrust the little gun barrel downwards, inside my sock and the inside top of my shoe, pulled the sock up and the trouser-leg down. I was about to close the bag when I caught sight of the two pairs of handcuffs. I hesitated, for on the form to date the likelihood was that, if I took them with me, they'd end up on my own wrists, but as it seemed too late in the day now to stop taking the chances that I'd been taking all along ever since I'd arrived in Amsterdam, I put both pairs in my left-hand jacket pocket and the duplicate keys in my right.

When I arrived back in the old quarter of Amsterdam, having left my usual quota of fist-shaking and police-telephoning motorists behind me, the first shades of early darkness were beginning to fall. The rain had eased, but the wind was steadily gaining in strength, ruffling and eddying the waters of the canals.

I turned into the street where the warehouse was. It was deserted, neither cars nor pedestrians in sight. That is to say, at street level it was deserted: on the third floor of Morgenstern and Muggenthaler's premises a burly shirt-sleeved character was leaning with his elbows on the sill of an open window, and from the way in which his head moved constantly from side to side it was apparent that the savouring of Amsterdam's chilly evening air was not his primary purpose for being there. I drove past the warehouse and made my way up to the vicinity of the Dam where I called de Graaf from the public phone-box.

'Where have you been?' de Graaf demanded. 'What have you been doing?'

'Nothing that would interest you.' It must have been the most unlikely statement I'd ever made. 'I'm ready to talk now?'

'Talk.'

'Not here. Not now. Not over the telephone. Can you and van Gelder come to Morgenstern and Muggenthaler's place now.'

'You'll talk there?'

'I promise you.'

'We are on our way,' de Graaf said grimly.

'One moment. Come in a plain van and park further along the street. They have a guard posted at one of the windows.'

'They?'

'That's what I'm going to talk to you about.'

'And the guard?'

'I'll distract him. I'll think up a diversion of some kind.'

'I see.' De Graaf paused and went on heavily: 'On your form to date I shudder to think what form the diversion will take.' He hung up.

I went into a local ironmongery store and bought a ball of twine and the biggest Stilson wrench they had on their shelves. Four minutes later I had the Opel parked less than a hundred yards from the warehouse, but not in the same street.

I made my way up the very narrow and extremely ill-lit service alley between the street in which the warehouse stood and the one running parallel to it. The first warehouse I came to on my left had a rickety wooden fire-escape that would have been the first thing to burn down in a fire but that was the first and last. I went at least fifty yards past the building I reckoned to be Morgenstern and Muggen-thaler's, and nary another fire-escape did I come to: knotted sheets must have been at a premium in that part of Amsterdam.

I went back to the one and only fire-escape and made my way up to the roof. I took an instant dislike to this roof as I did to all the other roofs I had to cross to arrive at the one I wanted. All the ridgepoles ran at right angles to the street, the roofs themselves were steeply pitched and treacherously slippery from the rain and, to compound the difficulties, the architects of yesteryear, with what they had mistakenly regarded as the laudable intention of creating a diversity of skyline styles, had craftily arranged matters so that no two roofs were of precisely the same design or height. At first I proceeded cautiously, but caution got me nowhere and I soon developed the only practical method of getting from one ridgepole to the next—running down one steeply pitched roof-side and letting the momentum carry me as far as possible up the other side before falling flat and scrabbling the last few feet up on hands and knees. At last I came to what I thought would be the roof I wanted, edged out to street level, leaned out over the gable and peered down.

I was right first time, which made a change for me. The shirt-sleeved sentry, almost twenty feet directly below me, was still maintaining his vigil. I attached one end of the ball of twine securely to the hole in the handle of the Stilson, lay flat so that my arm and the cord would clear the hoisting beam and lowered the Stilson about fifteen feet before starting to swing it in a gentle pendulum arc which increased with every movement of my hand. I increased it as rapidly as possible, for only feet beneath me a bright light shone through the crack between the two loading doors in the top storey and I had no means of knowing how long those doors would remain unopened.

The Stilson, which must have weighed at least four pounds, was now swinging through an arc of almost 90°. I lowered it three more feet and wondered how long it would be before the guard would become puzzled by the soft swish of sound that it must inevitably be making in its passage through the air, but at that moment his attention was fortunately distracted. A blue van had just entered the street and its arrival helped me in two ways: the watcher leaned further out to investigate this machine and at the same time the sound of its engine covered any intimation of danger from the swinging Stilson above.

The van stopped thirty yards away and the engine died. The Stilson was at the outer limit of its swing. As it started to descend I let the cord slip another couple of feet through my fingers. The guard, aware suddenly but far too late that something was amiss, twisted his head round just in time to catch the full weight of the Stilson on the forehead. He collapsed as if a bridge had fallen on him and slowly toppled backwards out of sight.

The door of the van opened and de Graaf got out. He waved to me. I made two beckoning gestures with my right arm, checked to see that the small gun was still firmly anchored inside my sock and shoe, lowered myself till my stomach was resting on the hoisting beam, then transferred my position till I was suspended by hands. I took my gun from its shoulder-holster, held it in my teeth, swung back, just once, then forwards, my left foot reaching for the loading sill, and my right foot kicking the doors open as I reached out my hands to get purchase on the door jambs. I took the gun in my right hand.

There were four of them there, Belinda, Goodbody and the two partners. Belinda, white-faced, struggling, but making no sound, was already clad in a flowing Huyler costume and embroidered bodice, her arms held by the rubicund, jovially good-natured Morgenstern and Muggenthaler whose beaming avuncular smiles now began to congeal in almost grotesque slow motion: Goodbody, who had had his back to me and had been adjusting Belinda's wimpled headgear to his aesthetic satisfaction, turned round very slowly. His mouth fell slowly open, his eyes widened and the blood drained from his face until it was almost the colour of his snowy hair.

I took two steps into the loft and reached an arm for Belinda. She stared at me for unbelieving seconds, then shook off the nerveless hands of Morgenstern and Muggenthaler and came running to me. Her heart was racing like a captive bird's but she seemed otherwise not much the

203

worse for what could only have been the most ghastly experience.

I looked at the three men and smiled as much as I could without hurting my face too much. I said: 'Now, *you* know what death looks like.'

They knew all right. Their faces frozen, they stretched their hands upwards as far as they could. I kept them like that, not speaking, until de Graaf and van Gelder came pounding up the stairs and into the loft. During that time nothing happened. I will swear none of them as much as blinked. Belinda had begun to shake uncontrollably from the reaction, but she managed to smile wanly at me and I knew she would be all right: Paris Interpol hadn't just picked her out of a hat.

De Graaf and van Gelder, both with guns in their hands, looked at the tableau. De Graaf said: 'What in God's name do you think you are about, Sherman? Why are those three men—'

'Suppose I explain?' I interrupted reasonably.

'It will require some explanation,' van Gelder said heavily. 'Three well-known and respected citizens of Amsterdam—'

'Please don't make me laugh,' I said. 'It hurts my face.'

'That too,' de Graaf said. 'How on earth—'

'I cut myself shaving.' That was Astrid's line, really, but I wasn't at my inventive best. 'Can I tell it?'

De Graaf sighed and nodded.

'In my way?'

He nodded again.

I said to Belinda: 'You know Maggie's dead?'

'I know she's dead.' Her voice was a shaking whisper, she wasn't as recovered as I'd thought. 'He's just told me. He told me and he smiled.'

'It's his Christian compassion shining through. He can't help it. Well,' I said to the policeman, 'take a good look gentlemen. At Goodbody. The most sadistically psychopathic killer I've ever met—or heard of, for that matter. The man who hung Astrid Lemay on a hook. The man who had Maggie pitchforked to death in a hayfield in Huyler. The man—'

'You said pitchforked?' De Graaf asked. You could see his mind couldn't accept it.

'Later. The man who drove George Lemay so mad that he killed him. The man who tried to kill me the same way; the man who tried to kill me three times today. The man who puts bottles of gin in the hands of dying junkies. The man who drops people into canals with lead piping wrapped round their waists after God knows what suffering and tortures. Apart from being the man who brings degradation and dementia and death to thousands of crazed human beings throughout the world. By his own admission, the master puppeteer who dangles a thousand hooked puppets from the end of his chains and makes them all dance to his tune. The dance of death.'

'It's not possible,' van Gelder said. He seemed dazed. 'It can't be. Dr Goodbody? The pastor of—'

'His name is Ignatius Catanelli and he's on our files. An ex-member of an Eastern Seaboard *cosa nostra*. But even the Mafia couldn't stomach him. By their lights they never kill wantonly, only for sound business reasons. But Catanelli killed because he's in love with death. When he was a little boy he probably pulled the wings off flies. But when he grew up, flies weren't enough for him. He had to leave the States, for the Mafia offered only one alternative.'

'This—this is fantastic.' Fantastic or not the colour still wasn't back in Goodbody's cheeks. 'This is outrageous. This is—'

'Be quiet,' I said. 'We have your prints and cephalic index. I must say that he has, in the American idiom, a sweet set-up going for him here. Incoming coasters drop heroin in a sealed and weighted container at a certain off-shore buoy. This is dragged up by barge and taken to Huyler, where it finds its way to a cottage factory there. This cottage factory makes puppets, which are then transferred to the warehouse here. What more natural--except that the very occasional and specially marked puppet contains heroin.'

Goodbody said: 'Preposterous, preposterous. You can't prove any of this.'

'As I intend to kill you in a minute or two I don't have to prove anything. Ah yes, he had his organization, had friend Catanelli. He had everybody from barrel-organ players to strip-tease dancers working for him—a combination of blackmail, money, addiction and the final threat of death made them all keep the silence of the grave.'

'Working for him?' De Graaf was still a league behind me. 'In what way?'

'Pushing and forwarding. Some of the heroin—a relatively small amount—was left here in puppets: some went to the shops, some to the puppet van in the Vondel Park—and other vans, for all I know. Goodbody's girls went to the shops and purchased those puppets—which were secretly marked—in perfectly legitimate stores and had them sent to minor heroin suppliers, or addicts, abroad. The ones in the Vondel Park were sold cheap to the barrel-organ men—they were the connections for the down-and-outs who were in so advanced a condition that they couldn't be allowed to appear in respectable places—if, that is to say, you call sleazy dives like the Balinova a respectable place.'

'Then how in God's name did *we* never catch on to any of this?' de Graaf demanded.

'I'll tell you in a moment. Still about the distribution. An even larger proportion of the stuff went from here in crates of Bibles—the ones which our saintly friend here so kindly distributed gratis all over Amsterdam. Some of the Bibles had hollow centres. The sweet young things that Goodbody here, in the ineffable goodness of his Christian heart, was trying to rehabilitate and save from a fate worse than death, would turn up at his services with Bibles clutched in their sweet little hands—some of them, God help us, fetchingly dressed as nuns—then go away with different Bibles clutched in their sweet little hands and then peddle the damned stuff in the night-clubs. The rest of the stuff —the *bulk* of the stuff—went to the Kasteel Linden. Or have I missed something, Goodbody?'

From the expression on his face, it was pretty evident

that I hadn't missed out much of importance, but he didn't answer me. I lifted my gun slightly and said: 'Now, I think, Goodbody.'

'No one's taking the law into his own hands here!' de Graaf said sharply.

'You can see he's trying to escape,' I said reasonably. Goodbody was standing motionless: he couldn't possibly have reached his fingers up another millimetre.

Then, for the second time that day, a voice behind me said: 'Drop that gun, Mr Sherman.'

I turned slowly and dropped my gun. Anybody could take my gun from me. This time it was Trudi, emerging from shadows and only five feet away with a Luger held remarkably steadily in her right hand.

'Trudi!' De Graaf stared at the young happily-smiling blonde girl in shocked incomprehension. 'What in God's name—' He broke off his words and cried out in pain instead as the barrel of van Gelder's gun smashed down on his wrist. De Graaf's gun clattered to the floor and as he turned to look at the man who had struck him de Graaf's eyes held only stupefaction. Goodbody, Morgenstern and Muggenthaler lowered their hands, the last two producing guns of their own from under their pockets: so vastly voluminous was the yardage of cloth required to cover their enormous frames that they, unlike myself, did not require the ingenuity of specialized tailors to conceal the outline of their weapons.

Goodbody produced a handkerchief, mopped a brow which stood in urgent need of mopping, and said querulously to Trudi: 'You took your time about coming forward, didn't you?'

'Oh, I *enjoyed* it!' She giggled, a happy and carefree sound that would have chilled the blood of a frozen flounder. 'I enjoyed every moment of it!'

'A touching pair, aren't they?' I said to van Gelder. 'Herself and her saintly pal here. This quality of trusting child-like innocence—'

'Shut up,' van Gelder said coldly. He approached, ran his hand over me for weapons, found none. 'Sit on the floor.

Keep your hands where I can see them. You, too, de Graaf.'

We did as we were told. I sat cross-legged, my forearms on my thighs, my dangling hands close to my ankles. De Graaf stared at me, his face a mirror for his absolute lack of understanding.

'I was coming to this bit,' I said apologetically. 'I was just on the point of telling you *why* you've made so little progress yourselves in tracing the source of those drugs. Your trusted lieutenant, Inspector van Gelder, made good and sure that no progress was made.'

'Van Gelder?' De Graaf, even with all the physical evidence to the contrary before him, still couldn't conceive of a senior police officer's treachery. 'How can this be? It *can't* be.'

'That's not a lollipop he's pointing at you,' I said mildly. Van Gelder's the boss, van Gelder's the brain. He's the Frankenstein, all right: Goodbody's just the monster that's run out of control. Right, van Gelder?'

'Right!' The baleful glance van Gelder directed at Goodbody didn't augur too well for Goodbody's future, although I didn't believe he had one anyway.

I looked at Trudi without affection. 'And as for your little Red Riding-hood, van Gelder, this sweet little mistress of yours—'

'Mistress?' De Graaf was so badly off balance that he no longer even looked stunned.

'You heard. But I think van Gelder has rather fallen out of love with her, haven't you, van Gelder? She has, shall we say, become too much of a psychopathic soulmate for the Reverend here.' I turned to de Graaf. 'Our little rosebud is no addict. Goodbody knows how to make those marks on her arms look real. He told me so. Her mental age is not eight, it's older than sin itself. And twice as evil.'

'I don't know.' De Graaf sounded tired. 'I don't understand—'

'She served three useful purposes,' I said. 'With van Gelder having a daughter like that, who would ever doubt that he was a dedicated enemy of drugs and all the evil men who profit by them? She was the perfect go-between for van Gelder and Goodbody—they never made contact, not even on the phone. And, most important, she was the vital link in the drug supply line. She took her puppet out to Huyler, switched it there for one loaded with heroin, took it back to the puppet van in the Vondel Park and switched it again. The van, of course, brought it here when it returned for more supplies. She is a very endearing child, is our Trudi. But she shouldn't have used belladonna to give her eyes that glazed addict look. I didn't catch on at the time, but give me time and clobber me over the head with a two-by-four and eventually I'll catch on to anything. It wasn't the right look, I've talked to too many junkies who had the right look. And then I knew.'

Trudi giggled again and licked her lips. 'Can I shoot him now? In the leg. High up?'

'You're a charming little morsel,' I said, 'but you should get your priorities right. Why don't you look around you?'

She looked around her. Everybody looked around him. I didn't, I just looked straight at Belinda, then nodded almost imperceptibly at Trudi, who was standing between her and the open loading doors. Belinda, in turn, glanced briefly at Trudi and I knew she understood.

'You fools!' I said contemptuously. 'How do you think I got all my information? I was given it! I was given it by two people who got scared to death and sold you down the river for a free pardon. Morgenstern and Muggenthaler.'

There were some pretty inhuman characters among those present, no doubt about that, but they were all human in their reactions. They all stared in consternation at Morgenstern and Muggenthaler, who stood there with unbelieving eyes and mouths agape and it was with mouths agape that they died, for they were both carrying guns and the gun I now had in my hand was very small and I couldn't afford just to wound them. In the same moment of time Belinda flung herself back against an off-guard Trudi, who staggered backwards, teetered on the edge of the loading sill, then fell from sight.

Her thin wailing scream had not yet ended when de Graaf reached up desperately for van Gelder's gun hand, but

209

I'd no time to see how de Graaf made out, for I'd pushed myself to my toes, still in a crouching position and launched myself in a low dive for Goodbody, who was struggling to get his gun out. Goodbody pitched backwards with a crash that spoke well for the basic soundness of the warehouse floors, which remained where they were, and a second later I'd twisted round behind his back and had him making strange croaking noises in his throat, because I'd my arm hooked around his neck as if I were trying to make the front and back ends meet.

De Graaf was lying on the floor, blood streaming from a cut on his forehead. He was moaning a little. Van Gelder led a struggling Belinda in front of him, using her as a shield, just as I was using Goodbody as a shield. Van Gelder was smiling. Both our guns were pointing at each other.

'I know the Shermans of this world.' Van Gelder's tone was calm, conversational. 'They'd never risk hurting an innocent person—especially a girl so lovely as this. As for Goodbody there, I don't care if he's shot as full of holes as a colander. I make a point?'

I looked at the right side of Goodbody's face, which was the only part of it I could see. Its colour varied between purple and mauve, and whether this was because he was being slowly strangled by me or because of his reaction to his erstwhile partner's ready and callous abandonment of him was difficult to say. Why I looked at him I don't know, the last thought in my mind was to weigh up the respective value of Belinda and Goodbody as hostages: as long as van Gelder had Belinda as a hostage he was as safe as a man in a church. Well, any church, that was, except the Reverend Goodbody's.

'You make a point,' I said.

'I make another point,' van Gelder went on. 'You have a pop-gun there. I have a police Colt.' I nodded. 'So, my safe-conduct.' He began to move towards the head of the stairs, keeping Belinda between us. 'There's a blue police van at the foot of the street. My van. I'm taking that. On the way there I'm going to smash the office telephones. If, when I reach the van, I do not see you at the loading door there, then I shall no longer require her. You understand?'

'I understand. And if you kill her wantonly, you will never be able to sleep easy again. You know that.'

He said, 'I know that,' and disappeared walking backwards down the stairs, dragging Belinda behind him. I paid no attention to his going. I saw de Graaf sitting up and taking a handkerchief to his bleeding forehead, so apparently he was still able to fend for himself. I released my throttling grip on Goodbody's neck, reached over and took his gun away, then, still seated behind him, brought out the handcuffs and secured both his wrists, one to the wrist of the dead Morgenstern, the other to the wrist of the dead Muggenthaler. I then rose, walked round to the front of Goodbody and helped a very shaky de Graaf to a chair. I looked back at Goodbody, who was staring at me with a face carved in a rictus of terror. When he spoke his normally deep, pontifical voice was almost an insane scream.

'You're not going to leave me like this!'

I surveyed the two massive merchants to whom he was chained.

'You can always tuck one under either arm and make good your escape.'

'In God's name, Sherman—'

'You put Astrid on a hook. I told her I would help her and you put her on a hook. You had Maggie pitchforked to death. My Maggie. You were going to hang Belinda on a hook. My Belinda. You're the man who loves death. Try it at close quarters for a change.' I moved towards the loading door, checked and looked at him again. 'And if I don't find Belinda alive, I'm not coming back.'

Goodbody moaned like some stricken animal and gazed with a horrified and shuddering revulsion at the two dead men who made him prisoner. I walked to the loading doors and glanced down.

Trudi was lying spreadeagled on the pavement below. I didn't spare her a second glance. Across the street van

Gelder was leading Belinda towards the police van. At the door of the van he turned, looked up, saw me, nodded and opened the door.

I turned away from the loading doors, crossed to the still groggy de Graaf, helped him to his feet and towards the head of the stairs. There, I turned and looked back at Goodbody. His eyes were staring in a fear-crazed face and he was making strange hoarse noises deep in his throat. He looked like a man lost for ever in a dark and endless nightmare, a man pursued by fiends and knowing he can never escape.

CHAPTER FOURTEEN

Darkness had almost fallen on the streets of Amsterdam. The drizzle was only light, but penetratingly cold as it was driven along by the high gusting wind. In the gaps between the wind-torn clouds the first stars winked palely: the moon was not yet up.

I sat waiting behind the driving wheel of the Opel, parked close to a telephone-box. By and by the box door opened and de Graaf, dabbing with his handkerchief at the blood still oozing from the gash on his forehead, came out and entered the car. I glanced up at him interrogatively.

'The area will be completely cordoned within ten minutes. And when I say cordoned, I mean escape-proof. Guaranteed.' He mopped some more blood. 'But how can you be so sure—'

'He'll be there.' I started the engine and drove off. 'In the first place, van Gelder will figure it's the last place in Amsterdam we'd ever think of looking for him. In the second place Goodbody, only this morning, removed the latest supply of heroin from Huyler. In one of those big puppets, for a certainty. The puppet wasn't in his car out at the castle, so it *must* have been left in the church. He'd no time to take it anywhere else. Besides, there's probably another fortune of the stuff lying about the church. Van Gelder's not like Goodbody and Trudi. He's not in the game for the kicks. He's in it for the money—and he's not going to pass up all that lovely lolly.'

'Lolly?'

'Sorry. Money. Maybe millions of dollars' worth of the stuff.'

'Van Gelder.' De Graaf shook his head very slowly. 'I can't believe it. A man like that! With a magnificent police record.'

'Save your sympathy for his victims,' I said harshly. I hadn't meant to speak like that to a sick man but I was

213

still a sick man myself: I doubted whether the condition of my head was even fractionally better than that of de Graaf. 'Van Gelder's worse than any of them. You can at least say for Goodbody and Trudi that their minds were so sick and warped and diseased that they were no longer responsible for their actions. But van Gelder isn't sick that way. He does it all cold-bloodedly for money. He knows the score. He knew what was going on, how his psychopathic pal Goodbody was behaving. And he tolerated it. If he could have kept the racket going on for ever, he'd have tolerated Goodbody's lethal aberrations for ever. I looked at de Graaf speculatively. 'You know that his brother and wife were killed in a car smash in Curaçao?'

De Graaf paused before replying. 'It was not a tragic accident?'

'It was not a tragic accident. We'll never prove it, but I'd wager my pension that it was caused by a combination of his brother, who was a trained security officer, finding out too much about him and van Gelder's desire to be rid of a wife who was coming between him and Trudi--in the days before Trudi's more lovable qualities came to the surface. My point is that the man's an ice-cold calculator, quite ruthless and totally devoid of what we'd regard as normal human feelings.'

'You'll never live to collect your pension,' de Graaf said sombrely.

'Maybe not. But I was right about one thing.' We'd turned into the canal street of Goodbody's church and there, directly ahead, was the plain blue police van. We didn't stop, but drove past it, parked at the door of the church and got out. A uniformed sergeant came down the steps to greet us and any reactions he had caused by the sight of the two crocks in front of him he hid very well.

'Empty, sir,' he said. 'We've even been up the belfry.'

De Graaf turned away and looked at the blue van.

'If Sergeant Gropius says there's no one there, then there's no one there.' He paused, then said slowly: 'Van

Gelder's a brilliant man. We know that now. He's not in the church. He's not in Goodbody's house. My men have both sides of the canal and the street sealed off. So, he's not here. He's elsewhere.'

'He's elsewhere, but he's here,' I said. 'If we don't find him, how long will you keep the cordon in position?'

'Till we've searched and then double-checked every house in the street. Two hours, maybe three.'

'And then he could walk away?'

'He could. If he was here.'

'He's here,' I said with certainty. 'It's Saturday evening. Do the building workers turn out on Sundays?'

'No.'

'So that gives him thirty-six hours. Tonight, even tomorrow night, he comes down and walks away.'

'My head.' Again de Graaf dabbed at his wound. 'Van Gelder's gun butt was very hard. I'm afraid—'

'He's not down here,' I said patiently. 'Searching the house is a waste of time. And I'm damned certain he's not at the bottom of the canal holding his breath all the time. So where can he be?'

I looked speculatively up into the dark and wind-torn sky. De Graaf followed my line of sight. The shadowy outline of the towering crane seemed to reach up almost to the clouds, the tip of its massive horizontal boom lost in the surrounding darkness. The great crane had always struck me as having a weirdly menacing atmosphere about it: tonight—probably because of what I had in mind—it looked awesome and forbidding and sinister to a degree.

'Of course.' de Graaf whispered. 'Of course.'

I said: 'Well, then, I'd better be going.'

'Madness! Madness! Look at you, look at your face. You're not well.'

'I'm well enough.'

'Then I'm coming with you,' de Graaf said determinedly. 'No.'

'I have young, fit police officers—'

'You haven't the moral right to ask any of your men,

young and fit or not, to do this. Don't argue. I refuse. Besides, this is no case for a frontal assault. Secrecy, stealth —or nothing.'

'He's bound to see you.' Unwillingly or not, de Graaf was coming round to my point of view.

'Not bound to. From his point of view everything below must be in darkness.'

'We can wait,' he urged. 'He's bound to come down. Some time before Monday morning he's bound to come down.'

'Van Gelder takes no delight in death. That we know. But he's totally indifferent to death. That we know also. Lives—other people's lives—mean nothing to him.'

'So?'

'Van Gelder is not down here. But neither is Belinda. So she's up there with him—and when he does come down he'll bring his living shield with him. I won't be long.'

He made no further effort to restrain me. I left him by the church door, crossed into the building lot, reached the body of the crane and began to climb the endless series of diagonally placed ladders located within the lattice framework of the crane. It was a long climb and one that, in my present physical condition, I could well have done without, but there was nothing particularly exhausting or dangerous about it. Just a long and very tiring climb: the dangerous bit still lay ahead. About threequarters of the way up I paused to catch my breath and looked down.

There was no particular impression of height for the darkness was too complete, the faint street lamps along the canal were only pinpoints of light and the canal itself but a dully gleaming ribbon. It all seemed so remote, so unreal. I couldn't make out the shape of any of the individual houses: all I could discern was the weathercock on the tip of the church steeple and even that was a hundred feet beneath me.

I looked up. The control cabin of the crane was still fifty feet above me, a vaguely seen rectangular darkness against a sky almost as dark. I started to climb again.

Ten feet only separated me from the trapdoor inset in

the floor of the cabin when a gap appeared in the clouds and a low moon shone through, a half-moon only, but the contrasting brightness bathed the yellow-painted crane and its massive boom in an oddly garish flood of light that highlit every girder and cross-member of the structures. It also highlit me and had the peculiar effect of making me feel as aircraft pilots feel when caught up in a search-light, of being pinned to a wall. I looked up again and could see every rivet-head in the trapdoor and the thought occurred to me that if I could see so well upwards anyone inside could see just as well downwards, and as the more time spent in that exposed position increased the chances of discovery I took my gun from its holster and crept silently up the last few steps of the ladder. I was less than four feet away when the trapdoor lifted a little and a long and very ugly-looking gun barrel protruded through the crack. I should, I know, have felt the chagrin and sickness which comes with the despair of the knowledge of ultimate defeat, but I'd been through too much that day, I'd used up all my emotions, and I accepted the inevitable with a fatalism that surprised even myself. It wasn't any question of willing submission, give me half a chance and I'd have shot it out with him. But I had no chance at all and I just accepted that.

'This is a twenty-four-shot riot gun,' van Gelder said. His voice had a metallically cavernous ring to it with sepulchral overtones that didn't seem at all out of place. 'You know what that means?'

'I know what that means.'

'Let me have your gun, butt first.'

I handed over my gun with the good grace and expertise that came from long experience of handing over guns.

'Now that little gun in your sock.'

I handed over the little gun in my sock. The trapdoor opened and I could see van Gelder quite clearly in the moonlight shining through the cabin windows.

'Come in,' he said. 'There's plenty of room.'

I clambered up into the cabin. As van Gelder had said, there was plenty of room, the cabin could have accommodated a dozen people at a pinch. Van Gelder, his usual calm and unruffled self, carried a shoulder-slung and very unpleasant-looking automatic gun. Belinda sat on the floor in a corner, pale-faced and exhausted, with a large Huyler puppet lying beside her. Belinda tried to smile at me but her heart wasn't in it: she had that defenceless and forlorn air about her that near as a toucher had me at van Gelder's throat, gun or no gun, but sanity and a swift estimate of the distance involved made me settle for lowering the trapdoor gently and straightening up in an equally circumspect manner. I looked at the gun.

'I suppose you got that from the police car?' I said.

'You suppose right.'

'I should have cheked on that.'

'You should.' Van Gelder sighed. 'I knew you would come, but you've come a long way for nothing. Turn round.'

I turned round. The blow that struck the back of my head was delivered with nothing like the vigour and the pride in his handiwork that Marcel had displayed, but it was still enough to stun me for a moment and bring me to my knees. I was vaguely conscious of something cold and metallic encircling my left wrist and when I began to take an active interest in what was going on around me again I found that I was sitting almost shoulder to shoulder with Belinda, handcuffed to her right wrist and with the chain passing through the metal hand grip above the trapdoor. I rubbed the back of my head tenderly: what with the combined efforts of Marcel and Goodbody and now van Gelder, it had had a rough passage that day and ached abominably just about wherever a head could ache.

'Sorry about the head,' van Gelder said. 'But I'd as soon have put handcuffs on a conscious tiger. Well, the moon's almost obscured. One minute and I'll be gone. Three minutes and I'll be on terra firma.'

I stared at him in disbelief. 'You're going down?'

'What else? But not quite in the way you imagine. I've seen the police cordon getting in position—but no one seems to have caught on to the fact that the tip of the crane

218

extends over the canal and at least sixty feet beyond the cordon. I have already lowered the hook to ground level.'

My head hurt too much for me to come up with a suitable comment: in the circumstances, there probably was none. Van Gelder slung his gun crosswise over one shoulder and secured the puppet with cord over his other shoulder. Then he said softly: 'Ah, the moon is gone.'

It was. Van Gelder was only a vaguely seen shadow as he crossed to the door let into the front of the cabin near the control panel, opened it and stepped outside.

'Goodbye, van Gelder,' I said. He said nothing. The door closed and we were alone. She caught my handcuffed hand.

'I knew you would come,' she whispered, then, with a flash of the old Belinda: 'But you did take your time about it didn't you?'

'It's like I told you—the managerial classes always have things to attend to.'

'And did you—did you have to say goodbye to a man like that?'

'I thought I'd better—I'll never see him again. Not alive.' I fumbled in my right-hand pocket. 'Who would have thought it? Van Gelder, his own executioner.'

'Please?'

'It was his idea to lend me a police taxi—so that I would be instantly recognizable and easily tailed wherever I went. I had handcuffs—I used them to secure Goodbody. And keys for the handcuffs. These.'

I unlocked the handcuffs, rose and crossed to the front of the cabin. The moon was behind a cloud, true enough, but van Gelder had overestimated the density of the cloud: admittedly, there was no more than a pale wash of light in the sky but enough to let me see van Gelder, about forty feet out now, the tails of his jacket and the gown of the puppet being tugged by the high wind, as he scuttled like a giant crab across the lattice framework of the boom.

My pencil flash was one of the few things that hadn't been taken from me that day. I used it to locate an overhead breaker and pulled the lever down. Lights glowed

219

in the control panel and I studied it briefly. I was aware that Belinda was now standing by my side.

'What are you going to do?' She was back at her whispering again.

'Do I have to explain?'

'No! No! You can't!' I don't think she knew exactly what I intended to do, but from what must have been some element of irrevocable finality in my voice she clearly guessed that the results of whatever action I took would be of a very permanent nature. I looked again at van Gelder, who was by now threequarters of the way out towards the tip of the boom, then turned to Belinda and put my hands on her shoulders.

'Look. Don't you know that we can never prove anything against van Gelder? Don't you know he may have destroyed a thousand lives? And don't you know he's carrying enough heroin with him to destroy another thousand?'

'You could turn the boom! So that he comes down inside the police cordon.'

'They'll never take van Gelder alive. I know that, you know that, we all know that. And he has a riot gun with him. How many good men do you want to die, Belinda?'

She said nothing and turned away. I looked out again. Van Gelder had reached the tip of the boom and van Gelder was wasting no time, for immediately he swung out and down, wrapped his hands and legs around the cable and started to slide, moving with an almost precipitate haste for which there was ample justification: the cloud band was thinning rapidly and the intensity of light in the sky increasing by the moment.

I looked down and for the first time could see the streets of Amsterdam, but it was no longer Amsterdam, just a toy town with tiny streets and canals and houses, very much like those scaled-down railroad models that one sees in big stores at Christmas time.

I looked behind me. Belinda was sitting on the floor again, her face in her hands: she was making doubly certain that she couldn't see what was going to happen. I looked towards the cable again, and this time I had no difficulty at all in seeing van Gelder clearly, for the moon had come from behind the cloud.

He was about half-way down now, beginning to sway from side to side as the high wind caught at him, increasing the arc of his pendulum with the passing of every moment. I reached for a wheel and turned it to the left.

The cable started to ascend, van Gelder ascending with it: astonishment must have momentarily frozen him to the cable. Then he clearly realized what was happening and he started sliding downwards at a much accelerated speed, at least three times that at which the cable was ascending.

I could see the giant hook at the end of the cable now, not forty feet below van Gelder. I centred the wheel again and again van Gelder clung motionless to the cable. I knew I had to do what I had to do but I wanted it over and done as quickly as was humanly possible. I turned the wheel to the right, the cable started to descend at full speed, then abruptly centred the wheel again. I could feel the shuddering jerk as the cable brought up to an abrupt standstill. Van Gelder's grip broke and in that moment I closed my eyes. I opened them, expecting to find an empty cable and van Gelder vanished from sight, but he was still there, no longer clinging to the cable: he was lying, face down, impaled on the giant hook, swaying to and fro in ponderous arcs, fifty feet above the houses of Amsterdam. I turned away, crossed to where Belinda sat, knelt and took her hands from her face. She looked up at me, I had expected to find revulsion in her face, but there was none, only sadness and weariness and that little-girl-lost expression on her face again.

'It's all over?' she whispered.

'It's all over.'

'And Maggie's dead.' I said nothing. 'Why should Maggie be dead and not me?'

'I don't know, Belinda.'

'Maggie was good at her job, wasn't she?'

'Maggie was good.'

'And me?' I said nothing. 'You don't have to tell me.' she said dully. 'I should have pushed van Gelder down the stairs in the warehouse, or crashed his van, or pushed him in the canal, or knocked him off the steps on the crane or —or—' She said wonderingly: 'He didn't have his gun on me at any time.'

'He didn't have to, Belinda.'

'You knew?'

'Yes.'

'Category Grade 1, female operative,' she said bitterly. 'First job in narcotics—'

'Last job in narcotics.'

'I know.' She smiled wanly. 'I'm fired.'

'That's my girl,' I said approvingly. I pulled her to her feet. 'At least you know the regulations, or the one that concerns you anyway. She stared at me for a long moment, then the slow smile came for the first time that night. 'That's the one,' I said. 'Married women are not permitted to remain in the service.' She buried her face in my shoulder, which at least spared her the punishment of having to look at my sadly battered face.

I looked past the blonde head at the world beyond and below. The great hook with its grisly load was swaying wildly now and at the extremity of one of the swings both gun and puppet slipped from van Gelder's shoulders and fell away. They landed on the cobbles on the far side of the deserted canal street, the riot gun and the beautiful puppet from Huyler, over which the shadow, like the giant pendulum of a giant clock, of the cable, the hook and its burden, swung in ever-increasing arcs across the night skies of Amsterdam.